ICONS

selected and introduced
by
Gordana Babic

with 64 colour plates

IP

Translated by Angus McGeoch

Icons

For centuries the icon has played a twofold rôle in European civilization: as an object of reverence and as a work of art. Orginally, the Greek word »eikon« never meant anything as straightforward as »picture«, a painted representation; it was a more abstract term, expressing the establishing of a resemblance, a reflection and reproduction of something living, an image of memory, which takes the place of the original subject which is no longer present or accessible.

In the Orthodox Church greater importance was attributed to icons than to any other pictorial expression of faith. In the Byzantine Empire, at the time of the Iconoclastic Controversy (726–843 A.D.) they were set above human life itself.

At the outset, when the Christian faith first made its appearance and began to spread through the Roman Empire, Christians did not recognize any pictorial representation, whether it be sculpture or any other material symbol of their spiritual convictions. They had a profound antipathy to the old-established pagan custom of deifying idols. There is not a single painting, relief or monument dating from before 200 A.D., which can be considered a Christian work of art.

In contrast both to the polytheistic pagan and to the mono-theistic Judaic tradition, as well as to the teachings of many Hellenistic philosophical and religious sects, the Christian dogma was preached in secret communities for a long time without recourse to any external symbols. The first Christian thinkers had founded their faith in absolute spirituality. Despite the delight in visual imagery found in the Mediterranean world, where strong traditions spurred talented artists to creativity, the Christians were for a long time opposed to the society around them and renounced the arts entirely.

The author Tertullian of Carthage (c.160–220 A.D.) who was a professing Christian, mentions a painter who adopted the new faith, but who from that moment on no longer earned his living from his artistic skill and had to make money in other ways. Other written sources also testify to the fact that artists were forbidden to take up the Christian faith, if they did not renounce the making of certain idols, since this activity was considered dangerous. The Christian dogmatists of the first half of the 3rd century, Origen of Alexandria and Methodius, the bishop of Olympia in Lycia, constantly stressed that God should be worshipped in a manner that required neither temple, nor altar, nor statues. Clement of Alexandria, the famous Christian writer (c.150 to before 215 A.D.) also energetically opposed any representation of the Christian God, because the true picture of Him was the Logos (the Word).

The scholarly theologians preferred the abstract concept of a God who dwelt in the realm of ideas, and denied any possibility that he could be recognized and represented through the medium of the human senses.

Yet less educated believers did not always remain faithful to the rigorous precepts of the theologians. The Apocryphal Gospels tell an interesting story about a portrait of St John the Apostle which was painted secretly and was taken by a school-boy named Lycomedes to his room, where he garlanded it with flowers, set it on an altar and lit candles in front of it.

The apostle rebuked the boy for this and called the painting a childish folly; but Lycomedes kept it and showed his gratitude to his benefactor according to the customs of that time, by worshipping his image.

This legend dates from the 2nd century and came from Asia Minor, where the adoration of a living person was transferred to their pictorial image. In the Life of St Pancratius, who was martyred as a Christian in 304 A.D., the relationship of one his Christian followers to the already deceased Pancratius, is described as follows: »… I ordered a picture of my teacher to be painted, and when I behold his revered visage in the painting, I believe that I see him before me in person.« Thus the early Christians began to use images in order to show gratitude to their benefactors or to conjure up the presence of one departed.

Around the year 200 A.D. and later in the 3rd century Christian tombs appear in ever greater numbers. On wall-paintings in the catacombs, in reliefs on sarcophagi, and even in 3-dimensional sculptures, stories from the Old and New Testaments are depicted, which teach the salvation of those who believe in Christ. Gradually Christianity began to adopt the figurative imagery of paganism to express biblical legends, and selected objects or figures (fish, ship, vine, the Good Shepherd etc) which served to illustrate aspects of dogma, or even to represent Christ himself. However, these first Christian works of art were in no way icons to be worshipped in specific places, but only didactic symbols, illustrations of man's salvation and eternal life in the kingdom of heaven, which were promised to believers after their earthly existence. The earliest representations of Christ and the saints were used more by individuals than by the Church, as a means of keeping alive the memory of long-dead founders of the new faith.

In 313 A.D., when the Roman emperor Constantine the Great (311–337) elevated Christianity to be the official religion of the empire, the Church found itself compelled to change the fundamental attitude of its followers towards art as such. When the Church took account of the new situation it recognized not only the Roman custom of deifying their emperors, but also the necessity of holding Christian services in public. The leaders of the Church then assigned to art its inevitable role in the life of the Christian community. From this moment on we find images serving the cult of emperor-worship alongside those glorifying the Christian faith. From the beginning of the 4th century onwards, architecture, applied arts and especially painting support all the efforts of the Church to educate its followers and to convert the pagans. With financial support from Constantine the Great and other powerful patrons, monuments were built on the sites of Christ's Passion and the martyrdom of his followers, and these were decorated with paintings, reliefs and a variety of sacred objects. Thus arose the shrines which attracted pilgrims in great numbers. Relics and sacred objects, which had come into contact with the mortal remains of saints, or pieces of the Holy Cross, were often taken away by visitors as valuable and frequently miraculous symbols of devotion.

The Church elders regarded these relics not only as objects designed to provoke religious ecstasy. For example, Gregory, the renowned author and bishop of Nissa in Asia Minor (d.394 A.D.), wrote in his obituary of the martyr Theodorus about those who were granted the good fortune themselves to touch a relic: »they have experienced this event with their eyes, mouth, ears and all their senses, and thus, shedding tears of gratitude and passion, directed their prayers for intercession to the martyr, as though he were present, alive and hale.« The bishop was thoroughly aware of the need for the faithful to receive impressions through their senses and to conjure up in their imagination the reality of the saints from whom they expected help. It was significantly easier to win people over to the Christian faith, using the sensual perception of this evidence of the supernatural power of Christ. The importance of perceiving a relic with the senses, which was stressed in Christian writings towards the end of the 4th century, also opened up the possibility of permitting Christian iconography, which would bring to mind the personages depicted and awaken a feeling of reverence toward them.

If we browse through the old legends and vitae, we might say that the images of Christ and the saints were principally regarded by the people as objects possessing supernatural powers. In particular it was to representations of saints and stylites that paranormal effects were attributed. Believers used them as magical objects, which for example were capable of warding off misfortune. Theodoretos, a religious author from Antioch (d.466), tells us that in Rome pictures of St Simeon were frequently hung over the doorways of workshops, since he was the patron saint of craftsmen. Superstition and vernacular tradition, deeply rooted in pagan times, gradually wove themselves around the relics brought back from the Holy Land. In this way the conviction spread that the saints had exceptional power which operated as much through their images as through their mortal remains. The Church tacitly approved of the belief in the evidence of biblical events, of the miracles performed by Christ or the Old Testament prophets, who had foretold the coming of Christ, and it permitted the adornment of the walls of sacred buildings with images of them. Nor did the Church oppose the spread of the myth of

the magical potency of relics brought back from pilgrimage shrines. In this way they endorsed both the didactic and the ritual role of icons; but for a long time the Church said nothing about their true identity. In 306 AD the Council of Elvira (near Granada in Spain) forbade the setting up of icons in churches, but this decision appears to have had only a limited local effect. For in the Eastern Empire the famous 4th century theologians, Basil the Great (330–379), Gregory of Nissa (d.394) and Gregory of Natiantia (329/30–390) took no account of the possible danger of idolatrous worshipping of early Christian works of art. Some scholars even justified the role of images in the development of religious sensibility; one such was Asterius of Amassia in Pontus (late 4th century), who admired the depictions of the martyrdom of St Euphemia, but expressed the view that Christ should not be represented in art. In the 5th century the monk Nilos advised Olympiodorus, who was endowing a church, only to decorate it with scenes from the Old and New Testaments and to place a crucifix above the altar. In the context of church decoration he does not mention any especially revered icons, so we can presume that at that time such images were not to be found in every church. From many writings which have come down to us we can conclude that the learned bishops throughout both the Eastern and Western Empires encouraged the didactic role of iconography. The mosaics which were created for the church of Santa Maria Maggiore, at the behest of Pope Sixtus III (432–440), bear witness to the already common decoration of walls with scenes from the Old and New Testaments. The processes, the technical knowledge and the compositional solutions of the experienced Hellenistic masters were applied in the design of Christian monuments, so that the thread of anthropomorphic art from the ancient world has been woven into the basic texture of Christian artistic expression.

The historical personalities of Christendom thus lived on in images, and while these evoked admiration among their devotees, they encountered the unyielding resistance of the traditionalists, who had remained true to the original dogma of the early Church. It was in in this century-long confrontation that the concept of the icon, a portable image to be venerated, gradually grew to maturity.

The celebrated church historian, Eusebius, bishop of Caesarea in Asia Minor (d.339 A.D.), wrote a letter to Constantia, the sister of the emperor Constantine, in which he refused the lady's request that he obtain a portrayal of Christ for her. He explained to her that God, despite his dual nature – divine and human – could not be pictorially represented, since the inanimate paints were incapable of expressing the spiritual essence of the Logos. Although this wish had been expressed by a person of great influence, Eusebius remained true to the intellectual principle of his faith, which was based on abstract concepts. In his attempt to to explain to Constantia the abstract nature of God, he compared Him to light: »How then could any man succeed in something that is impossible? How could a child of Man paint such a wonderful and incomprehensible form – if indeed one can give the name »form« to such a spiritually divine being. Unless in the manner of the pagans, without belief, he wished to paint something which bore no similarity, or a heathen artist was found, who painted everything quite differently... Who would be capable of representing, with uncertain brush-strokes and with soulless and lifeless paints, the sparkling and glowing rays of such sublimity and glory?... Hast thou forgotten God's commandment, which says: »Thou shalt not make for yourself any image nor any likeness, neither of that which is in heaven, nor of that in the water under the earth. (Moses II, 20.4) Hast thou ever heard, even from others, that any such thing was ever discussed in the Church? Is not all this condemned throughout the world and banished far from the churches...?«

In the years when he was writing his church history, Eusebius knew of certain works of art which depicted the cross as the symbol of Christendom, or personages from Christian history. He knew of the statue of Christ with the woman who had the bleeding flux in the town of Panea (Caesarea in Palestine); and of portrayals of the apostles Peter and Paul and the images of Jesus Christ; he knew that the emperor Constantine had ordered paintings for his palace in Constantinople depicting the prophet Daniel and the Good Shepherd (as the embodiment of the Lord); he knew that there was a cross in one of the rooms of the palace – the cross which had made possible Constantine's victory over Maxentius at the Milvian Bridge on the Tiber in 312 A.D. In place of the traditional trophies the emperor had thus hung up a cross as the symbol of victory and the celestial power of Jesus Christ. And during the campaign – so Eusebius tells us – he always put up his tent where the cross was being guarded, and prayed before it, hoping for its assistance. But although he did not expressly oppose the emperor's introduction of icons and Christian symbols into the sphere of court life, Eusebius remained a sceptic and a traditionalist, who stubbornly refused to accept the possibility of depicting Christ – regardless of the dual nature that was ascribed to Him, on the grounds that the divinity of Christ must alter his human nature.

Epiphanius, from the Cypriot town of Salamina (d.403 AD), fought even more fiercely against the »evil« of portraying Christ, the Mother of God, the martyrs, angels, apostles and prohets.«If you accept this painted image,« he said, » then the heathen customs have won the day,« and with that he tore up a canvas depicting Christ or a saint, which he had found in a village church. Epiphanius also wrote a letter of protest to the emperor Theodosius II (379-395), known for his opposition to pagan worship, in which he complained that artists painted what they had not seen, so that their paintings were pure lies. He besought the emperor to forbid all depiction in mosaic of apostles, prophets and of Christ himself. In his will, Epiphanius issued a warning to his contemporaries not to adorn either churches or the tombs of saints with pictures.

It was the clearly expressed opinion of the learned bishops of that period, that God could not be encompassed by art, and that icons, regardless of their Christian content, did not represent the truth, since they did not show anything that the artists had personally seen. Furthermore, the display of »unknown forms« to the public could well encourage the worship of dead objects – for the people still clung to pagan ways. Nevertheless, the complex development of the illustrative arts in the service of religion could not be halted, particularly since the emperor and the official Church appeared to give it every encouragement. What was still lacking was a theological explanation of the difference between an idol and a representation of the Christian God, even though both had been created with the same artistic resources. Even so, in the centuries that followed, the evolution of Christian worship was particularly assisted by icons. Yet the old conflicts lived on until 726 AD when, under the Byzantine emperor Leo III, the fight against the worship of icons was taken up officially. This »Iconoclastic Controversy«, as it is called, continued until 843 and ended with the permanent reinstatement of icon-worship, which had now found its justification in theology.

In early Christian times there were many influences from outside the teachings of the Church which contributed to the growth of iconography. This is especially true of the popular belief in the supernatural powers of relics or the depictions of martyrs, but its questionable whether these influences would alone have been sufficient, if the Church had not at certain points in time exploited them for its own purposes. As early as the 4th century, in the quest for a theoretical basis for the unity of Church and State, the notion was born of Christ as sovereign of the Christian universe, whose earthly representative was to be the Roman Emperor. It is true that at this time Constantine the Great held sway over most of the Mediterranean world; Eusebius of Caesarea speaks of him as the ruler of the world, naming the source of his power Panbasileus, the celestial authority. With the evocation of Christ as sovereign of the Christian universe a hierarchical power-structure was created, which permitted the Roman emperor to impose upon his subjects, and on the inhabitants of neighbouring countries, the idea of his absolute primacy. In turn it offered the bishops of the Christian Church the opportunity of giving a definite form to depictions of Christ, so that the same veneration could be shown to these as to images of the earthly emperor.

Constantine the Great divided the Roman Empire into a western and an eastern part, and in 330 A.D.transferred his official residence from Rome to Byzantium on the Bosphorus. He also decreed that 11th May should be celebrated annually as the date of the founding of »New Rome«, which was renamed »Constantinopolis« in his honour.

As late as the 6th century on this day the portrait of the emperor was still carried through the streets in a procession. And we know that people would kneel before his likeness and light candles as a sign of reverence; those accused of wrongdoing would seek asylum beside statues of the emperor and plead for his mercy and protection. Any damage done to a likeness of the emperor was punished, as if it had been done to the person of Constantine himself. This emperor-worship dating from pagan times was carried on into the Christian empire, since it was not possible to cease venerating the emperor, even when he had adopted Christianity. On the contrary, the veneration became more profound, and that was bound to have its effect on the glorification of Christ, the ruler of the Christian universe. However, the emergence of icon-worship was a process which took place very slowly and in different ways at various times and in various parts of the empire.

Another historian of the early Church, Philostorgius, who lived in Constantinople in the first half of the 5th century, writes of incense and candles, of prayers and talismans being offered up before the statue of Constantine in the forum of the imperial capital. In the same document he also describes a statue of Christ in Panea, but he makes no mention of any kind of worship. He adds that in the reign of the emperor Julian the Apostate (361-363 A.D.) the statue was removed from the town square and placed in the deaconry of the nearby church. From this we can conclude that the Christ-figure was not everywhere given the same veneration as the statue of the Roman Emperor. The emperor's portraits hung in courtrooms, market-halls, theatres and assembly-rooms, in fact in all public buildings. They were the embodiment of the emperor, who could not personally be everywhere at once, and they signified the concurrence of the citizenry with the actions of his representatives. Whenever a new emperor succeeded to the throne, his portrait was dispatched to every province, so that the citizens could declare their loyalty to him. Any refusal to show the usual forms of reverence was held to be a non-recognition of the new ruler and often led to armed conflict. Severianus of Gabala, in Syria, (d.after 408) states categorically: »The portrait of the emperor represents him in his absence... and the people honour him, since it is not his likeness but his person to whom they make obeisance.«

Severianus' declaration that the relationship to the image can be understood as the relationship to the person portrayed, in other words, that the image acts as an intermediary between the observer and the person to be venerated, was very important to the thinking of Christian theoreticians, because they later used this as a way of explaining the relationship to the portrayal of Christ, standing for Christ himself as the incarnation of God. Basil the Great (d.379 A.D.) the respected theologian from Cappadocia, was the first to claim that » the honour shewn to the image applies also to the origin of the image.« However, he made this statement in respect of the emperor's image. This interpretation had not yet been applied to representations of Christ; on the contrary, in the 5th century stress was predominantly laid on the magic power of the image of Jesus Christ.

The writer Ruffinus of Aquilea (d.410 A.D.) has also left us a description of the statue of Christ in Panea, but unlike Eusebius and Philostorgius, he mentions a miraculous plant, which helped to cure the sick, because it had sprung up close to the statue. Ruffinus thus confirms the already deeply-rooted belief among the people, that contact with a representation of God could work miracles.

Furthermore, Christ frequently appeared in visions and brought unexpected things to pass. In the words of the orator Zacharius (d.553 A.D.) who was also bishop of Mytilene and whose writings have been preserved in a Syrian chronicle, even the Persian king, Kavad, had such a vision: during the capture of the city of Amida on the Tigris, which up to that time (504 A.D.) had been in Byzantine hands, King Kavad found an icon of Christ in the crypt of the city's church and declared that Christ had already appeared to him in a vision, and had prophesied his victory.

In the written sources of the second half of the 6th century we find an increasing number of legends about miracles performed by icons of Christ and the Virgin Mary, as well as details of forms of icon-worship. Pagan beliefs, superstition and numerous ancient customs were grafted on to the rituals of the new religion. From the works of St Augustine (5th century), who openly opposed the portrayal of Christ, we learn that a woman called Marcellina paid equal homage to Christ, St Paul, Homer and Pythagoras and burned incense in front of their images. In writers and pilgrims of the 6th and 7th centuries we often find similar accounts of the use of incense. From this we must conclude that the ancient customs and forms of worship were transferred to icon-worship. Antonius of Piacenza writes around 570 A.D. of how, in the praetorium of Pontius Pilate in Jerusalem he paid homage to an image of Christ, and in Memphis (Egypt) he saw the first reproduction of the face of Christ, in the *sudarium*, or sweat-cloth, on which Our Lord's features had been preserved; *palium lineum in quo est effigies Salvatoris.* At about the same time, in Edessa on the river Tigris, the legend appears of a portrait that was not painted by human hand but by Christ himself. According to the author Evagrius Scholasticus (d.600 A.D.) the image is said to have saved Edessa when the city was besieged by the Persians in 544 A.D. This legend was repeated by Eusebius of Caesarea and Procopius (6th century), though in their versions there is no mention of it having been »painted by no human hand.« Apparently the learned Orthodox bishops of the late 6th century found it essential to provide explanations for icons as instruments of the will of God or the embodiment of supernatural powers. Such representations must therefore also have been created by supernatural means. Various explanations were offered in the form of legends, but the greatest success was achieved by the myth of icons of Christ and the Virgin Mary, that were »painted by no human hand,« but which must have come into being through direct contact with the holy personages they depicted, as was firmly believed. In the 6th century the pilgrim Theodosius travelled to the Holy Land to pay homage to the visage and the figure of Christ, which were said to be imprinted on the pillar in Jerusalem against which Jesus Christ was flogged. These imprints are also later mentioned by Antonius of Piacenza, from whose account it emerges that this relic, which was at the same time an imprint, had attracted the attention of the faithful. Naturally Palestine was rich in shrines of this kind, but at the same time other leading towns and monasteries gained in importance by acquiring similar rarities.

In about 530 A.D. the teacher Theodorus tells us that Eudoxia, the wife of the emperor Theodosius II, sent from Jerusalem a picture of the Virgin Mary reputedly painted by St Luke the Evangelist, to Pulcheria, daughter of the emperor Arcadius, who lived in Constantinople until 453 A.D. Icons of this kind, which people believed to be true likenesses and to have been touched by saints, stood in high esteem. But in the course of the 6th century, when in the vast and renewed Roman Empire under Justinian I (527-565 A.D.) many devout preachers strengthened the Christian faith and numerous churches were built, there was an ever greater need for such icons.

In this period myths spread about the self-duplication of the original image, since the need was growing for a sensual perception of the Godhead. »How shall I worship him, if he is invisible and I know him not,« asks a woman in the 6th century Syrian chronicle. Her wish was fulfilled: in her well she found an image of Christ on linen, and when she wove this miraculous object into her cloth, the image reproduced itself in a copy, which the myth claimed was *acheiropoietos* – »not made by human hand.« In order to protect this icon a church was built in Kamuliani in Asia Minor. The picture continued to duplicate itself and between 554 and 560 A.D. a copy of it was carried in a procession through the cities of Asia Minor, in order to raise money for the rebuilding of a church that had been torn down. The practical exploitation of icons was encouraged by the chronicler, in order to draw the attention of his readers to a very widespread parallel between the arrival of the icon in that town and the Second Coming of Christ on earth. All the details of the ceremonial remind one of the formal welcome and the arrival (*adventus*) of the emperor returning in triumph from a victorious campaign.

Both the bishops and the temporal authorities learned very early on how to exploit the popular belief in the magical power of images. The Byzantine chronicler Theophilus Symokata (early 7th century) tells us that as early as 586 A.D. a general named Philippicus, in the battle on the river Arzamon against the Persians, ordered a banner to be raised bearing an image of Christ that was »not painted by human hand«, in order to inspire new courage into his troops. A little later we are told, by the early 7th century Byzantine poet Gregorius Pisada, that the emperor Heraclius (610-641) ordered a similar miraculous icon be carried at the head of his troops in the campaign against Persia. This was probably the Kamuliana icon – or a copy of it – which had been brought to Constantinople by Justinian II in 574 A.D.

And during the siege of Constaninople in 626, when the Persians were already closing in on the city from the east, and simultaneously Avars, Slavs, Bulgars amd other »barbarians« were attacking from the European side, the much revered icons of the city were brought out to give encouragement to the defenders. One who witnessed these events, Theodorus Sinculus, noted that the Patriarch Sergius (610–638) ordered that at nightfall images of the Mother of God with Christ should be placed at every gate in the western fortifications. Later, when the city was put to the torch, Sergius personally carried the miraculous icon of Christ along the walls, while praying aloud and urging the defenders of the city to resist the enemy. Another contemporary, Gregorius Pisida, also testifies to these events.

Using icons to influence the credulous masses at critical moments in a war clearly proved successful, for during later sieges of Constantinople, for example in 717–8 A.D., when the Arabs attacked the city, an icon of the Virgin Mary and a relic of the Holy Cross were borne along the fortifications. And just as the Roman emperors had once displayed their trophies to the legions, so did the rulers of the Christian Byzantine empire, the patriarchs and bishops, present icons as symbols of their victorious power, guaranteed by divine will. The general belief in the divine origin of worldly power was exploited in Byzantium – as it had previously been in the Roman empire – as a certain means of imposing political authority. That is why the cult of icons took on an ever more official character. The obeisance that was once only made to imperial images was now transferred to representations of Christ, and this ubiquitous cult-image came to occupy a larger and larger place in public life, in war and peace, in the Church and at court.

Not only in Constantinople and the eastern provinces of the empire, but also in Rome the icon of Christ that was »not painted by human hand« was carried about in Rogation Day processions.

From the middle of the 6th to the early 7th century the icon of Christ is mentioned more and more frequently in written sources. Under Justinian I, the great champion of Christianization, the icon had clearly gained a solid significance for the Church in the newly consolidated empire, which stretched from Cordoba and Gibraltar to the Tigris and Euphrates rivers, and from the Alps and the Danube as far south as the upper Nile valley. Justinian ordered the renovation of the Hagia Sophia church in Constantinople from the ground up, and offered artists the opportunity to give expression to the whole of Christian thought, especially on the altarpiece, which was to become the most important medium for their representations. In 529 A.D. Justinian ordered the closure of the Academy in Athens, where pagan scholars and neo-platonists were still giving lectures, and thus fell the last bastion of ancient Greek philosophy. Yet the dogmatic conflicts of the early Church, which had already been debated at the ecumenical councils of the 4th and 5th centuries, continued to shake both Church and State in the re-established empire with ever greater vehemence. In addition to the disputes about the conception of the divine and human nature of Christ, which none of the Justinian councils were able to resolve, there now emerged ambitions of political separatism in individual provinces and important ecclesiastical centres – Rome, Alexandria, Antioch – while at the same time the imperial government was anxious to secure the authority of the Patriarch in Constantinople. The decision of the Council of Chalcedon (451) concerning the two »indissociable but distinct« natures in Christ was by no means the only reason for new conflicts to break out. The primacy of the Pope in Rome was recognized, yet the almost equal rights of the bishops of Old and New Rome caused ever greater tension in relationships within the Church. The Monophysites in Syria, Egypt and Armenia refused to accept the dogma of Chalcedon. They stressed the unique – and divine – nature of Christ and pursued a policy of opposition to the central authority of Constantinople.

The Byzantine emperors became directly involved in all ecclesiastical disputes, being fully aware of their political implications and anxious to preserve their own absolute authority.

The policy of the emperor and his relationship to the dogmas of the Church left visible traces in the art of the period, especially with regard to the icon of Christ. Research has shown that the earliest legends about the icon of Christ »not made by human hand,« date from the second half of the 6th century. This indicates that they must have originated in that period, when numerous heresies and constant attacks by the Persians were weakening imperial authority, and every effort was made to gain the loyalty of the representatives of the eastern provinces. For these icons worked miracles, specifically in Kamuliana, Edessa, Amida and Memphis – in other words precisely those areas where the reinforcement of the Byzantine notion of the representation of Christ as the Word made flesh seemed to be most necessary. The Patriarch Sergius and Emperor Heraclius made various attempts to find an interpretation of the dogma which would satisfy both Constantinople and Rome as well as the eastern provinces. First they put forward the theory of the two natures but the one and indivisible power of Christ. Then Sergius made the proposal that Christ had two natures but only one divine will. This interpretation was accepted by the emperor as well, and thus the new religious edict was proclaimed in 638 A.D. under the porch of St Sophia's church in Constaninople.

Yet even this attempt to unify the Church was unsuccessful; Rome rejected the edict and at the same time the Arabs occupied the eastern provinces. Then, as the Byzantine rulers were forced to accept ever more defeats on the battlefield and their empire was visibly shrinking, the emperors increasingly stressed their devotion to the cause of Christ. It is true that they no longer held sway over a vast empire, for the Arabs had captured Mesopotamia, Armenia, Cappadocia, and Egypt, and by 711 A.D. the whole of North Africa was under Arab domination. Nevertheless, they continued to stress the divine source of their power and defended their position as Christ's representatives on earth. The state ideology of Byzantium in that period was identified with the glorification of Christ, and the spread of the cult of icons was vigorously encouraged.

Christ was even represented on the coins of Justinian II (685–696 and 705–711) with the title *Rex Regnantium*, while on the other side the emperor was shown as *Servus Christi*. Unlike the Church in Constantinople, which encouraged the cult of icons, the eastern provinces displayed ever more open opposition to the use of »images« and put up resistance against the metropolis.

The doctrine of the Jews and Moslems, who refused to allow any human representation in their houses of worship, only aggravated the controversy about icons. As late as the end of the 7th century monks in Armenia fought stubbornly against the displaying of images in their churches. As an answer to their attacks an apologetic text was published containing the maxim: »...we recognize the invisible through the visible.« Finally the Church intervened in its turn to defend the use of icons and the anthropomorphic representation of Christ: the Council of Constantinople, held in 692, decided that painters should no longer depict Jesus pointing to the Lamb, but that in future He was to be shown in human form, as this would remind the faithful of his martyrdom and death and the salvation of mankind which this made possible.

The former principle of ancient art, the anthropomorphic presentation of abstract ideas, was now being officially adopted by the Christian world, though only in its eastern European part, whereas Rome remained aloof and the eastern provinces clung to their doctrine that it was impossible to express pictorially the abstract nature of God. In the 8th century this ideological conflict between east and west led to the ruthless destruction of works of art.

We must, however, remember that in Byzantium, even before the outbreak of the Iconoclastic Controversy in 726 A.D., images were frequently destroyed if they did not accord with the dogma that was currently being preached. When the Arians were banished from the Church, they burned the statue of the Patriarch and the icon of the Virgin Mary with Christ, which were in Constantinople in the reign of Constantius II (337-361); when the emperor Anastasius (491–518) adopted the doctrine of the one nature of Christ, he summoned a painter from Syria, an adherent of Manichaeism, to Constaninople to paint works in the imperial palace and the church of St Stephen. These paintings were completely at odds with the traditional iconography of Christ and created an uproar amongst the people. And when the emperor Bardanus Philippicus, the Armenian (711-713) declared the monophysite doctrine once again to be the single definitive doctrine of the Byzantine Church, he destroyed the picture of the 6th Ecumenical Council that hung in the imperial palace, because its members had condemned monothelism; he even had an inscription mentioning the Council removed from the city gate, and restored the pictures of the Patriarchs Sergius and Honorius to their rightful places. In Rome Pope Constantine I declared his position in the same manner: he banished the likeness of the heretical emperor Philippicus, which was no longer to appear in coins, nor was his name to be uttered in church services. Furthermore, as an unambiguous protest he had pictures of all six Councils displayed in St Peter's.

The displaying and removal of portraits as a symbolic mark of a particular dogmatic or political partisanship had been a Byzantine custom for centuries. The emperor Leo III (716–740) marked a turning-point in the Byzantine empire, when he had himself proclaimed simultaneously emperor and high priest, and attempted to turn the people away from all veneration of icons. At his behest the image of Christ was removed from the bronze door of the palace where it had been hanging; but this action unleashed rioting in the streets of Constantinople. This popular defiance proved how deeply the cult of icons was already rooted in human consciousness. The Patriarch of Constantinople, the Pope in Rome and the European part of the empire put up a fight against this policy of Leo III, who was seen as a lover of Islamic culture. The unambiguous speech of the emperor against icons in 726, and the Edict of 730, marked the beginning of a struggle which was to last more than a century between Church and State, between those who venerated icons and those who abhorred them, and between the eastern and western parts of the empire. The quarrel broke out first of all between the Emperor and the Patriarch, then spread through all levels of society and finally required the scholars of theology to defend their convictions in open forum.

The early doctrines of Philostorgius and of Pseudo-Dionysus the Areopagite (5th century) about the nature of icons and their relationship to their original archetype did not gain general acceptance until the 8th century. One of the first people to grasp the full import of the conflict between the eastern and the European traditions in the concept of images was John Damascenus (c.675–749). His words initially went unheeded, since he lived beyond the borders of Byzantium in Palestine, which by that date was already under the rule of the Arab caliphs. As the representative of the Christian community at the court of Sargun Ibn Mansuras in Damascus and later as a monk in the monastery of St Sava near Jerusalem, Damascenus finally, in the years 726–730, formulated an explanation of images which met the requirements of Christian dogma: »Icon signifies resemblance, a model of something reprsented...Certainly the image does not resemble its prototype in every regard... for the icon is one thing and that which the artist intended to depict is something else and it must be understood that there is a difference between the two...The image of a man for example shows the particular characteristics of his body, but it is not endowed with his intellectual faculties...« And in answer to the question as to the purpose of an image Damascenus answers: »Every image reveals something hidden. By that I mean that it is not possible for mankind to have direct knowledge of what is invisible (for his spirit is enclosed in his body); since man has not the power to see the future nor that which is very distant because he is subject to the limits of time and space, the image has been conceived in order to lead him into the way of knowledge and to reveal to him what is concealed...«

Without regard to the arguments of those who defended the cult of icons or to the beauty of the works of art, Leo III decreed that all icons should be removed from churches and private houses, taken to the main square of Constaninople and there burned. This was followed by executions, exile and other punishments...

In 754 the Iconoclastic Council was held at Hieria near Constantinople, and with the involvement of the emperor Constantine V it was decided that the divine Logos should not be represented by pictorial means. The Pope and the Patriarchs of the eastern provinces did not take part in this council. The Byzantine exarchate of Ravenna had fallen to the Lombards in 751 and so the Pope decided to make an alliance with the Frankish king, Pippin, and break away from Byzantium. This policy of the Roman Pope made it possible for artistic activity to develop undisturbed in Rome, while the east was being torn apart by the iconoclastic crisis.

While the empress Irene ruled during the minority of her son Constantine VI, the Council of Nicaea was called in 787 A.D., at which the defenders of the cult of icons decided that: »revered and sacred images, regardless of whether they are painted or worked in mosaic or any other suitable material, may be displayed in churches, on holy vessels and vestments, on walls and floors, in houses and beside highways; and these icons may not only be of Our Lord and Redeemer Jesus Christ but also of the Immaculate Virgin, the Mother of God, the holy angels and all the saints and men of righteousness. For the more often such painted representations are contemplated, the sooner will those who observe them call to mind their original subjects, will devote themselves to them in order, by kissing them as humble sinners, to show them the reverence due to them; this is however no ordinary adoration... since the veneration shown to the icon passes through it and ascends to the original archetype.«

On this declaration rests the doctrine of the Iconophiles and the later followers of the Patriarch Methodius, the emperor Michael III in his minority and his mother Theodora, who in 843 A.D. proclaimed the restoration of the worship of icons.

Few icons have survived from this earliest period of Christian art. Most of the evidence comes from regions which were a long way from Constaninople, where the Iconophiles had greater influence: in Rome, in the Coptic monasteries of Egypt, in St Catherine's Monastery in Sinai, and in Georgia, on the eastern shores of the Black Sea, which had been reached by Christianity as early as the 3rd century. Thus the oldest icons that have come down to us date from the 6th and 7th centuries. They portray Christ, the Virgin Mary, the apostles and the saints. The figures of Christ and of the first witnesses of his supernatural powers in the icons of the 6th century stress certain physical characteristics; they are clad in particular garments and hold specific objects in their hands: the book of Gospels, for example, the cross, or a phylactery. They are adorned with a halo and are recognizable by precise gestures. They stand or sit immobile, with their exaggeratedly large eyes staring fixedly at the observer. Depicted as occupying a realm beyond space and time, they betray no emotion, they play no part in earthly life, they do not move, nor teach, nor suffer. Only with their expressive eyes – which had always been considered to be mirrors of the soul and the spirit – do they convey the artist's longing to be closer to eternity and thus to God. If the portrayal of saints and martyrs relied on certain iconographic principles, the representation of Christ, Mary and the Apostles returned constantly to dogma and tradition. We know that the earliest pictures of Christ differed greatly from each other; some portrayed him as a young man, others as old, some gave him the appearance of a Zeus, others presented him as a Greek sage. However, in the 6th century the image that predominated in icons was that of Panbasileus, of Pantocrator, the Lord of the entire Christian universe, and of the Saviour – in middle age, calm, stern and wise.

In a 6th century Coptic icon (tempera on wood, now in the Louvre, Paris) Christ is designated as SOTIR (Saviour) and St Mynas beside him as intercessor or representative of the faithful before Christ the Saviour (PATIR MYNAS PPOEITOS, i.e. Father Mynas Intercessor). In the purely two-dimensional portrayal of the bodies, and their small and insignificant size, in the broad, large-eyed faces and the cool ochre and olive tones of this picture one can see the typically oriental desire to express something abstract and to ignore or avoid all the laws of beauty which the Greeks and Romans, pagan and Christian, were governed by in the first centuries of the present epoch.

We may assume that the ancient concept of the Beautiful is most lastingly reflected in the icons which were created in Constantinople. Several examples of this stylistic trend were preserved in the monastery of St Catherine in the Sinai peninsula. In the 19th century they were taken to Berlin and Russia and can be seen today in Kiev. They are encaustic, painted in the traditional technique of Mediterranean artists, who mixed their paints with hot wax. John the Baptist stands with a written scroll of vellum (John I, 29), portrayed as an ancient sage, perhaps an orator, with the whole weight of his body resting on one foot and pointing with an expansive gesture to to the figure of Christ in the medallion. Christ is shown with the Virgin Mary (as *imagines clipeatae* of the emperor and empress on the diptych of the console), so that the concept of St John and the Virgin Mary as intermediaries in the salvation of mankind is brought home clearly to the observer. With powerful brushstrokes and thickly applied paint the outlines of the prophet's body are clearly visible under the folds of his dark brown robe, while the observer's attention is drawn by his arresting, wide-open eyes and the full lips under the thick hair of his beard and moustache. The plasticity of the picture achieved by the colours reveals the artist to be a devotee of the ancient notion of the beauty of the human body, and tells us that he was very familiar not only with the techniques but also with the stylistic principles of the ancient masters.

The same qualities in the depiction of bodily forms, albeit in lighter and livelier colours, can also be found in the icons of the Madonna and Christ-child (also in Kiev), and the portrayal of St Peter from the Sinai collection, which also includes the famous Madonna and Christ-child, with saints and angels, while one of he most beautiful examples of encaustic icons in this collection depicts the head and shoulders of Christ (Pantocrator) with the Gospel. All these icons have been preserved far from their original location, so that their real purpose is unknown. Some are quite large, others smaller in size, but we do not know whether they were they object of collective worship in a church or were hung in a private house or monk's cell for personal veneration. However, all of them – including the famous encaustic icon of SS. Sergius and Bacchus (6th cent. Kiev) – bear witness to an iconography already firmly established, as shown by the prescribed appearance of the leading figures of Christendom, and the mutual relationship of benevolence and assistance, which Christians expected of them.

The icons of the saints clearly express the rôle of intercessor, which Christian believers ascribed to them. Mankind turned to Christ to plead for salvation, but chose the path of intercession through The Virgin Mary, St John, the martyrs and saints. For this reason they appear as full-length figures, present in the flesh in the altarpieces, whereas Christ is only shown in a medallion as the image of someone absent (*imago clipeata*), in the same way that the emperor is shown, for example, beside the consul who is portrayed as a complete figure on ivory diptychs. The oldest icons from Constantinople are characterized by their imperial Byzantine iconography and the specific interpretation of the human form inherited from the ancient world.

As early as the 6th and 7th centuries we can recognize in Roman icons certain characteristics which would only be developed in the later history of western art. The Roman church began at a very early date to represent the Virgin Mary as the Queen of Heaven. In the encaustic icon known as La Madonna della Clemenza, which is preserved in the church of Santa Maria in the Trastevere quarter of Rome, the Madonna wears a crown richly ornamented with precious stones and pendants, and a purple dalmatic with decorations at the neck, and holds a cruciform sceptre in her hand. With the Christ-child on her lap, she sits on a throne while two angels keep watch beside her. This mixture of immobility and movement, of solemn tones in the Virgin's finery and lively colours in the robes of the angels, as well as the contrast between the impassive face of the Queen of Heaven and expressive features and animated faces of the angels – all these are the marks of a new style which was gradually being borrowed anew from the neglected portraiture of the artists of antiquity.

Very different characteristics are seen in the icons from the Sinai collection, which are thought to have originated in Palestine: the forms reduced to two dimensions, the strongly expressive draughtsmanship and the dispensing with any kind of spatial perspective give a wholly foreign appearance, for example, to the icons depicting St George and St Theodorus on horseback. The absence of any information whatsoever about the artist or the place of origin of these and many other icons has caused researchers and art-lovers to be cautious and reticent in drawing any conclusions. It is nonetheless certain that there were numerous workshops in monasteries and at the imperial court producing these portable and deeply venerated sacred objects. Icons were carried from one end of the empire to the other, as costly gifts, and as indispensible adjuncts to

worship to which reverence was made and from which mercy and salvation were sought. For high-ranking individuals icons were made in a small size, often as a diptych, tryptich or polyptych from ivory, silver, enamel, steatite, bone or wood. Although few icons have survived from the early period of Byzantine art, we can assume that the most valuable ones came from the workshops of Constantinople itself. However, in the distant lands of the Caucasus astonishing art treasures have survived, which give us some idea of the brilliance and beauty of these earliest icons. Especially noteworthy are the silver-clad images from the 9th to 12th centuries. There also exist iconostases (altar-screens) or fragments of them dating from this period, as well as (masonry altar-screens) from the 11th century. The tall Geogian altar-crosses clad in gold or silver which reflected the sun's rays penentrating the dome. In making their icons and crucifixes the skilled Caucasian artists copied the ancient technique of chasing – the art of hammering out figures on sheets of silver and then fixing them to a wooden base.

The wealth of the patrons who commissioned and donated these works of art, intended to furnish churches or private houses, made it possible for this tradition of art and craftsmanship to survive for many centuries. The continuing efforts of the artists to bring to life the legends of the saints in silver plate, with the help of the iconography of eastern Christianity and the traditional canons of composition, led to a remarkable precision in their workmanship and to a rare formal beauty in the icons of the 11th to 13th centuries.

The artists of the Caucasus were inspired not only by the generally known and revered saints of Christendom but also by their local patron saints. For example, St George was frequently represented as a mounted warrior (as he was in other Christian countries), but the legends of the Georgians saw him as a hero who killed the emperor Diocletian (284–305 A.D.) with a lance as he fell under the horse's hooves. In Georgia Diocletian was held to be a symbol of evil, the embodiment of all the foes of Christendom; the renowned and saintly warrior therefore had to be shown triumphing over him. This form of representation lasted right into the 18th century, when the great tradition of sacred art finally deteriorated into naive folk-art.

Although they observed the basic artistic principles of eastern Christianity the artists of Georgia introduced into the traditional compositions and iconographic models certain variations which – especially in the 9th and 10th centuries – clearly differentiated them from the artistic activity of Constantinople in the same period. The strongly stylized lineaments of the two-dimensional folds of the drapery as well as the elongation and simple outlines of the figures (most frequently those of Christ and the Madonna) emphasize the symmetry of the composition, and the calm and awe-inspiring solemnity of the facial expressions. Since human anatomy was ignored in favour of geometric stylization, the human figures acquire a monumental appearance. This is even true of the small icons from the churches of Tchukuli. Tchitchareshi etc. The silver-chased 10th century icons from the churches of Peka, Gelata, Lagurka and Martvili exhibit an individual trend in style which was followed throughout the Caucasus region.

In this period the Georgian artists were already putting their signature to many of the icons. Their works were highly prized and rewarded; their fame spread quickly and soon they were respected members of society. The links between Georgia and Byzantium in the late 10th and 11th centuries led to a deeper and deeper interpenetration of artistic influences and ever more frequent borrowing of formal elements from the art of Constantinople. This process was repeated in the 12th and 14th centuries, when both patrons and artists again paid closer attention to developments in the capital of the Byzantine empire. The Georgian Orthodox Church followed the decrees of the Patriachate of Constantinople, retained the traditional form of church service and continued to decorate the altar-screens, whereas in Armenia the Monophysite doctrine gained the upper hand, so that icons and decorated altar-screens disappeared from Armenian churches. Benefactors almost invariably commissioned illuminated manuscripts and donated them to the church.

That is why it is predominantly in the monuments of the countries of the Caucasus, and Georgia in particular, that the most talented artists created priceless icons, which today enable art-historians to discern and interpret the stylistic developments and forms of design of the various centres of artistic activity.

Our knowledge of the oldest icons and altar-screens from Constantinople is partly based on information from written sources. In the verses of Paul Silentiarius, which were read aloud in St Sophia, Constantinople, in 563, the splendour of the icons on the altar-screen of this important metropolitan church, are described in general terms. Although the descriptions are lacking in detail, the modern reader can still gain a strong impression of the beauty of the pictures on the screen which divides the altar from the *naos* or nave, the part of the church where the congregation stands. The architrave was supported by twelve columns and three doors opened into the chancel. The panels in the lower part of the screen and the columns and architrave were all plated with silver so that the blazing rays of light illuminated the entire width of the church. Engraved on the architrave were medallions in which the images of Christ, the angels, prophets, apostles and the Virgin Mary appear as *imagines clipeatae*, while the central panels carried medallions of the cross as well as the monograms of the emperor Justinian I and the empress Theodora. This is the only description that we possess of this magnificent altar-screen, which divided the two parts of the church as if they were two different worlds, the temporal and the spiritual. The concrete representation of this symbolic frontier between the realms of the spirit and of matter, the realm of the here-and-now from the kingdom of eternity, shows us that even in the 6th century art and the liturgy had found a means of expressing the fundamental principle of Christian doctrine, that of redemption of the faithful, and of prayer and intercession by the Virgin and the apostle John (represented among the prophets) on behalf of the congregation before their Judge and Saviour. The prophets had predicted the kingdom of Christ on earth, and the apostles had preached it, which is why they were depicted on the screen which led to the mystical world of the glorious Kingdom of Heaven. One can judge the wealth and generosity of those who donated this screen when one compares it with those that have survived from other churches of this or later periods, which are made from stone, metal, ceramics, brick or wood. Nonetheless,

regardless of the richness or simplicity of the materials used, the forms always carry the same message expressed by Justinian's court poet in his description of the altar-screen in St Sophia's. Everything depicted points to the possibility of gaining the Kingdom of Heaven where Christ Pantocrator reigns, to whom the Virgin Mary and St John carry the prayers of his flock.

Every Orthodox church has an iconostasis, or altar-screen. Many have survived, though the majority were destroyed, which is why our knowledge of their development remains imprecise and incomplete. In 4th century churches the screens were so low that they hardly reached above the knees of the priest and enabled the congregation to follow the rituals of the Mass and Eucharist. In the eastern empire they became higher as time went on. In the post-Byzantine period they completely close off the chancel and deprive the uninitiated visitor to the church of their view of the altar. In the course of the 18th and 19th centuries decoration disappears from the walls of the church, while it grows more and more opulent on the iconostases. The iconostasis is now the only medium carrying images and reliefs in the interior of Orthodox churches.

The increasing custom of hanging icons of different subjects on to altar-screens began in the Middle Ages. The interruption of the development of figurative or symbolic decoration by the Iconoclastic Controversy continued to have repercussions in many provinces of the empire, despite the triumph of orthodoxy in 843 A.D.; in fact, the opponents of icons – Paulicians, monophysites and others – still hoped to return to the days of the iconoclastic emperors (Leo III, Constantine V, Leo IV, Leo V, Michael II and Theophilus). The patriarch Nicephorus (805-815) testifies to the removal of symbolic ornamentation from altar-screens, curtains, pelmets, columns and doors, when he spoke of the depiction of beasts and monsters, »for they served only to adorn and beautify«. However, the embellishment of the stone and wooden pelmets, capitals and architraves of the screens persisted and increased. Icons gave the altar-screens their first real significance.

As long as the periods of turmoil and conflict endured, the forms of ornamentation where obviously not identical in every province of the Byzantine empire. In individual cases the local bishops used their discretion. But when icons finally achieved general recognition, they established a basic ideological agenda: the Deisis, or representation of the fundamental law of intercession with Christ in judgement by the representatives of mankind, (the Virgin Mary and St John), occupied the central position on the iconostasis. Whether these images were carved on stone or metal architraves, painted on panels called »templons« along the architrave, or executed individually and arranged in the correct order, in the earliest period they always had the same theme of intercession by the saints on behalf of mankind. To the basic motif of the Deisis with its three figures (*trimorphon*) might be added angels, evangelists or a number of apostles (known as the Great Deisis or Deisis with ritual) and even, at a later date, the depiction of a martyr or a saint, who had been chosen by the founder of the church or by the donor of the iconostasis as a personal protector or as patron saint of the church. In the imagery on stone altar-screens of the 8th and 9th centuries ther patrons saints submit their pleas to Christ for the salvation of their followers. The figures of these saints are usually carved in medallions on the stone beams, but sometimes also in high-relief beneath highly decorative arcades. On the icons they were invariably framed since each one was an especially prized picture, the object of a special cult, and thus had to kept separate from its surroundings.

We have evidence from the post-iconoclastic period about screens and icons made from a wide variety of materials: in the church of the Saviour in Constantinople the emperor Basil I commissioned the building of a costly altar-screen, whose »columns and lower parts were made entirely from silver, while the cross-beams lying on the capitals were made of pure gold and set with all the treasures of India. The image of Our Lord, the Son of Man, was reproduced in enamel in several places on the cross-beam…«

From this description we can assume that the architrave in the church of St Basil was already decorated with scenes from the Gospels, of which only Christ, as the most important participant, is mentioned. Other evidence points to the conclusion that from the 10th century onward another series of icons representing scenes of the great religious festivals began to adorn the architraves of altar-screens, above or beside the Deisis. In that period especially revered icons were also placed to the right or left of the altar-screen on walls or pillars. They were also given specially ornamented frames, either of painted wood or stone and looking like relief-style frescos.

These icons represented Christ, the Virgin Mary, or the two of them together, as well as a particularly revered saint. The iconography which earlier was only displayed on the architrave thus spread to the side-walls and pillars of the altar-screen (e.g. in St Sophia's church in Nicaea, in the Protaton on Mount Athos and the Panagia of Phocida – all from the 10th century). A few fragments from some richly decorated screens of this period have survived; for example, a white marble slab with small encrusted panels of multicoloured stones, paste and glass (opus Alexandrium), which dates from the 10th century and represents St Eudoxia; it comes from a church in Constatinople endowed by Constantinus Lipsus, a senior imperial official. In the Byzantine Museum in Athens there is a marble panel – part of a templon dating from around 900 A.D., on which can be seen encaustic portraits of three apostles inlaid in the stone.

Stone altar-screens with figurative decoration (Deisis and the benefactor's patron saint) dating from the 9th century have been found in churches in Asia Minor (fragments in the museum in Afion-Karahissar) and in southern Greece (Thebes, the island of Chios), which lead to the conclusion that at that time Constantinople was once more influencing the work of artists in those provinces where there was less resistance to the restoration of icon-worship. In places that had no great wealth and lacked access to artists skilled in working in mosaic, enamel and incrustation, the benefactors from provincial towns and villages commissioned artists to paint pictures on the walls. These pseudo-icons, which were not portable, were given carved stone or painted wooden frames in imitation of genuine icons. For example, in St Sophia's church in Ohrid (mid-11th C.) the two pillars of the former altar-screen have fresco-icons of the Madonna and Child as a symbolic representation of the divine wisdom to which the church was dedicated. In the altar-screen of Nerezi (1164) of which nothing remains but the huge fresco-icons of the Madanna and Child and of St Panteleon, on the

side pillars, the columns, the architrave and the frame of the fresco-icons were made of marble. Stone-masons of great talent must have carved this impressive frame, and their patron may well have been a member of the imperial family. In the cave-church of St Neophyte in Cyprus (late 12th C.) both the altar-screen and the icons were made of wood. On the other hand, in the church of the Holy Archangels in Iprari (Georgia, 1096) in the cave-church of St Sophia on Kithara (12th C.) and in the so-called Evangelistarium in Geraka (Peloponnese, third quarter of 12th C.) the screens were built of brick and painted with frescos. From these frescos it can be seen that from the 11th century onward the fresco-icons filled the spaces between the colonettes. Thus the religious services were largely held behind the partly closed altar-screens. We learn from written sources that the abbot Desiderius of Monte Cassino (1058–1086) was sent from Constantinople a templon with six silver colonettes and ten icons for the new altar-screen; five icons were hung on it beneath the architrave. The typokon, or rule-book, of the monastery of Bačkovo (1081) laid down that oil-lamps should be lit at specified times in front of the icons of St George and the Crucifixion on the altar-screen. In St George's church in the fortified town of Geraka (12th–13th century) painted icons of the Virgin Eleusa and Christ Pantocrator have survived on plaster panels between the marble colonettes of the screen, while fresco-icons of the Holy Warriors have been painted on the side pillars.

Even when the icons were painted on wood and then fixed to the altar-screen, in the lower part of the screen they continued for centuries to proclaim the original religious message. All the images on altar-screens were dominated by the cross which was the symbol of Christ's sacrifice and the sign which began and ended every prayer. The late 12th century painted cross which has survived in Sinai is evidence of a once detailed depiction of the Passion of Christ at the top of the altar-screen. This custom was continued on painted altar-crosses in Italy until well into the 13th century, while in the Orthodox churches of the Balkans the narrative of the Passion was incorporated into the basic representation of the crucifixion. The famous carved and painted crosses which have come down to us from the 16th to 18th centuries, on Mt Athos and in the Balkans, use the figures of Christ, the Virgin Mary and St John the Evangelist or the body of Christ crucified, to stress only the bare outline of the events, and the actual image of the crucifixion, which is also the focus of the liturgy.

Icons, cross, curtains and the main door to the altar (with the Annunciation to the Virgin, and later other themes as well) – all these are components of the screens which now concealed the secret parts of the liturgy according to a fixed ritual. Greek bishops passed on the art of writing, Christian forms of worship, books and icons to the Bulgars, who were converted in 863 A.D., the Russians of Kiev (988 A.D.) and to other Slav and Balkan cities and peoples. In the 11th and 12th centuries the powerful influence radiating from the Church in Constantinople opened new perspectives for cult objects and sacred art. From the metropolis valuable icons reached as far as Novgorod in the north and Ohrid in the south. Even the precise places where they were to be displayed were carefully prescribed. In Georgia and Russia, in the Balkans and Italy the same forms were adhered to in the decoration of altar-screens in the 11th century. Later this uniformity of design was lost. In the east the altar-screens became larger and blocked off the Holy of Holies with icons and curtains, whereas in the west the icons were withdrawn to the high altar, the screen became lower and the ritual of the liturgy was opened up to the congregation.

In Italy, where the use of icons gradually altered after 1054, the influence of Byzantine painting can nevertheless be detected up to the end of the 13th century. The Italian Madonnas of this period from Lucca and Florence betray to what models they owe their origin. In the work of the Berlingheri family of painters (c.f. the Madonna in the Strauss collection, New York) or in the work of the Florentine Master of Bigallo, the debt owed to migrant Byzantine artists can clearly be seen.

But certain features of Romanesque paintings can also be traced. The tendency towards ornamentation, to arabesques and intertwining lines, distinguishes the Italian painters of madonnas from the Byzantine icon-painters. The attempt, through the posture and gaze of the Madonna, to establish a certain relationship between her and the observer, is quite foreign to the eastern artists, for they were trying to indicate a world beyond, a celestial world. For example the painter of the Madonna and Christchild with angels (Sinai, mid-12th century) uses a mass of gold lines, in order to bathe his figures in the glittering light of the background and reduce the impression of material reality; on the other hand, the contemporary Italian master, Coppo di Marcovaldo, though he also uses whole sprays of gold lines, does so in order to emphasize the roundnesses of the body shapes in his picture, and at the same time aims to achieve plasticity, to make the three-dimensionality more obvious: the golden texture becomes a delightful ornament. The strength of the influence of Byzantium on the painting of the crusaders, who ruled Constantinople from 1204 to 1261, as well as on Greek and Italian art, can be seen from the icons of the lives of saints. This form of painting, which originated in the ancient world and was much used in Byzantium and many other Christian countries in the Middle Ages, shows the saint, to whom the icon is dedicated, in the large central space, while the episodes from his life appear in a sequence of tiny scenes around the edge. In the Balkans, Cyprus, Italy and Georgia, this form of art was cultivated at various times but always under Byzantine influence. Until well into the 18th century artists in the Balkans and Russia painted their favourite patron saints in this manner, most often St Nicholas (the patron saint of seafarers) St George (the patron saint of farmers) and the Virgin Mary. When Serbian painters depicted the life and miraculous deeds of St Sava, the first Serbian archbishop, they composed the picture according to the old-established formula. One such icon, which shows Sava with his father, St Simeon Nemenja, founder of the Nemenjid dynasty and the first member of the Serbian church to be canonized, has been preserved in the monastery of Morača and dates from 1645. In Russia, where the Greek saints had long been depicted in this way, the people also venerated local miracle-workers such as Boris and Gleb (Moscow, Tretyakov Gallery, 14th C.), and Alexis, Archbishop of Moscow (late 15th C.) In Italy St Francis of Assis was revered (icons from Assisi c. 1270; from Pisa c. 1260–70), St Catherine (icons from Pisa, mid–13th C.) and others. In Byzantine iconography and in the art of those peoples who took Byzantium as their model, there are many other forms of composition and design, which – like these icons – testify to a heritage taken over from the ancient world and a long respected and thriving tradition.

Over the centuries Constantinople had assumed the role of guardian of a great cultural tradition. The imperial libraries, the artists' workshops, the architectural monuments and artistic legacy made up a priceless treasure-house, from which artists drew knowledge and inspiration to meet the needs of their own times. Yet despite this great variety, one factor had always been supremely important in Byzantine painting: the striving to find an abstract ideal, a prototype. In order to conjure up this *Urbild* the artists disguised their human figures, in order to prevent too much reality from intruding; to make the effect more spiritual, they elongated the proportions of their subjects, deprived them of weight and corporeal curves, and lit them from behind with the splendour of gold and the radiance of vermilion or pale ochre. The complete accordance between abstract ideal and spiritualized human form, which carried a religious message, was at its most convincing in the late 11th century icons of the capital of the Byzantine empire.

In the 11th century a great number of icons must have been painted, not only for the new and renovated churches and monasteries of the capital, but also for the numerous newly created bishoprics, through which the Patriarchate of Constantinople extended its sphere of influence, especially among the Slavs and Bulgarians. In Ohrid an icon of the »Forty Martyrs« has survived from this period. This is a relatively rare subject, but the 11th century frescos in the north chapel of St Sophia's church provide evidence that the cult of these warrior-martyrs was particularly popular in the archbishopric of Ohrid. The freezing to death of the near-naked heroes on the frozen Lake Sebaste, their contempt for death and their unshakeable faith in their ideal are the principle themes of this depiction.

The icon-painter glorifies the renunciation of all earthly things, while he attempts to sketch the figures, reduced to their basic outlines, and to suggest the men's pain and suffering with the minimum of detail – furrowed brows, rings under the eyes, heads sunk in a swoon, hands folded on the chest, placed against the cheeks or raised in prayer to Christ.

In different periods various human qualities were ascribed to the martyrs and saints, Christ and the Virgin; these found their clearest expression in the second half of the 12th century and around 1300, when for the last time Constantinople exerted an influence on artisitic activity throughout the length and breadth of Orthodox lands. Under the rule of the Comnene and Paleologue dynasties the serene harmony that had been achieved in 11th century was abandoned. Now, every means was sought to emphasize the authenticity of the emotions and sufferings and the reality of the events depicted. In the icons of this period Christ and those who witnessed his presence on earth, are imputed with qualities which make them more similar to normal mortals. In the 11th century the other-worldly calm of these figures made the distance between the Christian believers and their ideal even greater. But now, although the themes of the pictures had not changed, a range of emotions were evoked by them in the observer. There are countless representations of Mary and the Christchild but every artist has woven into his picture his own ideas and his vision of faith and life, and has used his paints to repeat the eternal theme in his own fashion. In this way the anonymous icon-painters are able for the first time, despite their traditional stylistic vocabulary, to display their own individual talent and – like all true artists – become accessible to today's world.

Russia's oldest centres of icon-painting grew up in the 11th and 12th centuries. In the St Sophia church and the Lavra Pecherska monastery in Kiev artists must have been producing a large number of icons as early as the second half of the 11th century.

It is possible to get an idea of the earliest shrine in Kiev simply from a miniature contained in the so-called Trier Psalter (today kept in Cividale). The book was embellished with miniatures in about 1078-1087, when it was in the possession of Princess Gertrude Izyaslav of Vishgorod. The miniature shows the Virgin with the Christchild; she is sitting on the throne, gazing to the front with a sublime solemnity. The few surviving icons from Russian workshops of the 12th century are distinguished by the calm repose, the fixed gaze of the unnaturally large eyes of the saints, and by their striking symmetry. The ideal of 11th century Byzantine painting must for a long time have appealed to the piety of Russian patrons. The famous Madonna, known as the »Great Panagia« (now in the Tretyakov Gallery, Moscow) illustrates how the Russian icon-painters expressed the sublime beauty of these sombre figures painted against a gold background. The oldest and most beautiful Russian icons of this period were painted in Kiev, Vladimir, Yaroslav and Novgorod, before the Mongol invasions. The basic technique and knowledge of iconographic formulae were borrowed from Byzantine masters, but the Russians soon made use of their new-found skills to create and develop a purely native art.

We learn from early annals that a number of icons of the Virgin Mary were brought to Kiev from Constantinople. One of these has survived. Prince Andrei Bogolyubsky took it with him when he left his father in Kiev and returned to his birthplace, the city of Vladimir in the principality of Suzdal. He had the icon embellished with gold, silver, pearls and precious stones. Following the custom of the Byzantine emperors he made it the talisman of his nation, carried it with him into battle and made obeisance to it in the Greek manner. In 1395, when the Mongol conqueror Tamurlane withdrew his troops from the capital of this Russian principality, the icon was taken to Moscow. It was named after its previous resting-place »The Virgin of Vladimir« and today it can be seen in the Tretyakov Gallery. During the Middle Ages it was widely renowned; later Russian icon-painters often copied it, because the ancient belief persisted that similarity with the original could perpetuate the efficacity of its miraculous powers. It is true that only the middle section of the original picture has survived: the head of the Virgin with the the Christchild at her cheek. Centuries of adding and removing the silver fittings, hangings, overpaintings and miscellaneous damage have significantly altered the other parts of this oldest surviving Russian icon, since it first left its home in Constantinople.

Next to Kiev, Vladimir was the most important centre for the development of Russian art in the 12th century. Prince Vsevolod of Vladimir spent his youth in Constantinople, his son Konstantin spoke fluent Greek, and the prince's brother Mikhail founded a library in Vladimir containing over a thousand Greek manuscripts. The surviving icons of the Vladimir-Suzdal school are of exceptional beauty and demonstrate a complete understanding of the Greek concept of the icon as a reflection of the celestial, of the infinitely reproduced likeness, which assures its value and through which it is possible to attain the *Urbild*. Sublime tranquility, a background of glowing gold and symmetrically composed figures – these are the distinguishing features of Russian icon-painting until the Mongol invasion in the 13th century.

Even in this earliest period a whole range of subjects were created, which give the Russian icon-painters the status of artists in their own right, despite all their reliance on Constantinople. As early as 1071 Boris and Gleb were canonized by the Church. The veneration of these two sons of Prince Vladimir of Kiev, who were slaughtered on the orders of their own brother, spread very rapidly. Their icons were painted some time in the 12th century and in the year 1200 the Archbishop of Novgorod, Antoniye, made a pilgrimage to Constantinople to pay tribute to their images in the city's St Sophia church. This episcopal travel-chronicler from distant Novgorod reported that pilgrims could buy icons of Boris and Gleb in St Sophia. Their unfamiliar garb – caftan, cloak, fur hat and red leather boots – distinguished them from all known Greek saints and made them easily recognizable.

During the reign of the Latin emperors in Constantinople (1204–1261), and the Mongol domination in Russia, cultural links between Russian and Byzantine painters were severed. And even after that, when art began to flourish again in Byzantium, there seems to have been a long delay before Russia adopted anything new. Not until 1338 is a Greek painter named Isaia mentioned in Novgorod, while in Moscow a group of Greek artists worked under the patronage of the Metropolitan Teognost. However, all the evidence suggests that the new style of the Paleologue renaissance was only hesitantly introduced in Russia. The icons, frescos and miniatures of this style are distinguished by the plastic depiction of figures in lively movement and a clear spatial perspective. Furthermore, the number of people in each scene increased in order to lend the events portrayed more colour and visual persuasiveness. Finally, the icon-painters used light draftsmanship and inverted perspective to emphasize the actuality of the scenes which took place in the distant days at the beginning of Christian history. This style, which originated in Constantinople, was readily adopted by artists and their patrons throughout the eastern sphere of Christendom.

It was particularly in the Serbian lands that this new manner of composition quickly became popular; for art had begun to develop here since the end of the 12th century thanks to the commissions of wealthy local patrons. The icons that have survived from the late 13th and early 14th century testify to a concept of art that Constantinople shared with Salonika and Ohrid or the court of King Milutinus. The representations of the Virgin Peribleptos, of the apostle Matthew and others are works of true genius, admired and venerated by the people of Ohrid and many visiting pilgrims. Icons that were collected in Ohrid and those painted there for local patrons are still preserved in that city today in considerable numbers, proving that in the late 13th and the first half of the 14th century Ohrid must have been an important centre of artistic activity. Archbishops and feudal lords presented their churches with images painted by the best artists of that period. Some hung on the altar-screens in Ohrid's churches, and others on special supports which in 14th century Constantinople were known as »icono-stases.« (Later this term was applied to the altar-screens themselves). Yet others were hung or placed on consoles. The Patriarch of Antioch, Makarios, travelled in the mid-17th century with his son, Archdeacon Paul of Aleppo, who has left us an interesting account of their journey into the depths of Russia. In Novgorod's St Sophia church and in many churches in Moscow they saw book-like shrines, plated in silver or gold, in which either six or twelve icons were preserved, depending on whether they were painted on one or both sides of the page. They portrayed the saints for whom Masses were said during the year. Every month the sexton took the appropriate icon from the shrine and placed it on the analogion, as the console was called. A candle burned continuously in front of this icon. »…Such caskets can be found in every church, and not just one, but three or four of them, of various sizes and shapes. They are kept in front of the altar on the shelves of the analogion under a special cloth.« This eye-witness account by Paul of Aleppo supports the view that this custom was already widespread before the 17th century in Russia and in other countries. Many icons have not yet been analysed, and so we cannot be sure whether they were part of an altar-screen; but they may in fact have been intended for religious festivals and placed on the analogion. Since the calendar is painted on them, they can be taken as evidence for the worship of saints that are less generally known.

Only the very famous, miracle-working icons are given a topographical name in addition to their description; for example, the Virgin of Vladimir, of the Don or of Byelosersk in Russia, the Pelagonitissa in Macedonia, the Virgins of Studenica and of Hilandar in Serbia, and the Hagiosoritissa and Blachernitissa in Constaninople. This way of naming the most important shrines was probably common everywhere and in all periods. However, in the period of Paleologue art epithets for the Virgin and Christ appear, which stress their affinity with mankind and their capacity for emotion, for example: »Virgin full of Solicitude,« »Dispenser of Grace,« »Guide and Leader,« »Provider of Nourishment,« »Source of Life,« »Virgin of the Intercession,« »Redemptress,« »The All-Seeing,« »She who Eases our Pain,« the Virgin »Worthy of All Praise,« »the Merciful,« etc.

By crediting selected saints with certain attributes the independent national churches and individual donors introduced into the existing world of Christian iconography characteristics typical of their own particular society.

Towards the end of the Middle Ages painters were working for an ever growing number of patrons, not only for monarchs and rulers but for feudal lords, nobles and bishops. On icons from the Balkans in the 13th, 14th and 15th centuries the artist's signature is to be found with increasing frequency. The emergence of the painters from their former anonymity was a consequence of the changed attitude to their rôle in society, regardless of whether they were monks or lay artists.Thus, for example, the painter John (c.1266) from Ohrid in Macedonia

signed his icons, as did The Metropolitan John and his brother Makarios in the late 14th and early 15th centuries. We know the names of many masters from Russia, but the most famous of them was Theophanos the Greek, who in the 14th century left Constantinople for Novgorod and Moscow, where at that time numerous patrons supported a thriving artistic community. Theophanos did not sign many of his works but we know more about him from old chronicles. He worked on the altar-screen in the Moscow Kremlin along with Prohor of Gorodac and Andrei Rublyev, and in the church dedicated to the Annunciation. He also painted many frescos, icons and miniatures for individual Russian patrons. Andrei Rublyev, mentioned above, was a monk from the monastery of the Holy Trinity, founded by Sergius of Radonesh. In contrast to the Byzantine tradition of his monastic workshop, to which Theophanos remained loyal, Rublyev's work are recognizable by their sensitivity, soft modelling and pure lines on very pale areas of colour. And this light, lyrical palette was to be an enduring feature of Russian painting in the 15th century. Rublyev worked with his companion Daniel, who entered the monastery with him. His fame spread quickly, so that he soon became a model for later generations of painters. In 1551 a church assembly decreed: »…that the painters should paint their icons after the old exemplars, just as the Greek masters and Andrei Rublyev painted them.«

At the end of the line of successful Russian icon-painters stands Dionysios. His works date from the heyday of the principality of Muscovy under the rule of Ivan III (1462–1505), when many independent territories were absorbed into this strongest region of Russia. Following the decline of Byzantium and the final capture of Constantinople in 1453, Moscow itself was hailed as the »third Rome.« Russia imposed its leadership on all Orthodox countries, as the heir and successor to the Byzantine empire. In 1492 Metropolitan Zosim of Moscow named Prince Ivan III »lord and sole monarch of all the Russias,« and the »new emperor Constantine,« and named Moscow »the new city of Constantine.« The bloodline of the princes of Muscovy was traced back to the Roman emperor Augustus, and this was the foundation of their claim to the title of Tsar. In this period the Russian capital was an important centre of artistic endeavour. Many churches were furnished with icons. Dionysios worked for the royal court and was considered the best painter of his age. He had complete mastery of the old principles and evoked the *Urbild* with light, disembodied figures in pale colours and a soft, lyrical palette.

An echo of the Italian renaissance became detectable around 1500 in the icons of the so-called Italo-Byzantine style from the island of Cyprus. From the end of the 12th century Cyprus was ruled by Frankish kings (1192–1489), then by Venice and later the Turks. The powerful influence of Constantinople in the late 14th century on icon-painting in Salonika, Serbia and Russia, extended also to Cyprus, where the basic elements of Orthodox icon-painting were preserved until later ages. Scattered centres of art – in Serbia, Mistra, Moldavia, Mount Athos and in Russia – evolved particular qualities of design, but continued to respect the ideals and iconography established in Constantinople.

After the Turkish invasion of the Balkans and the fall of Serbia in 1459, the class of wealthy patrons disapppeared and the number of great artists also became smaller and smaller. During the 16th century icons were addmittedly still being painted in every Orthodox country, but their quality depended on the level of education of the donor and the artist, and the eastern world lagged behind the progressive thinkers and artists of Italy. In the 16th and 17th centuries the icon-painters of eastern Europe and the Greek islands (Crete, Mount Athos) remained wholly committed to the thousand-year-old ideal of the Neoplatonists and Byzantine theologists and seldom took over pictorial elements from Renaissance or Baroque art.

Nevertheless the taste of patrons in the Mediterranean world had to be satisfied, and in the 16th century Italo-Greek painters on Cyprus were already expressing many characteristics of their age in secondary, decorative details or in the garments worn by the benefactor kneeling before his patron saint. In the works of the famous Venetian masters who had congregated around the Greek monastery of St George, the compromise between Byzantine and European art in the 17th century finally destroyed the original ideal of the icon. The attempt to use perspective to depict landscape and the real relationship between man and Nature was at odds with the fundamental concept of the icon. The paintings of the well-known Graeco-Italian masters of the 17th century – Theodore Pulakis, Emmanual Zanfurnari, Victor the Cretan, Elias Moschos and their forerunners, Andreas and Nicholas Ricos – are no more than a series of tragically unsuccessful efforts to bring two worlds into unison – worlds whose aesthetic and ideological standpoints were diametrically opposed to each other. The monks on Mount Athos sensed the emergence of this new pictorial concept, for that secluded Greek monastery was where the so-called Italo-Cretan or Italo-Greek painters of the 16th and 17th centuries often did their work. But the Russians also experienced it as a genuine collision between old and new. From the description that has come down to us by Paul of Aleppo it is clear to see how disturbing these ideological and aesthetic conflicts were for the church fathers and artists of Moscow. In 1654 the Patriarch Nikon, reacting against the invasion by this new concept of art, decreed that all icons: »...which certain Muscovite icon-painters have started to paint in imitation of Polish and west European examples,« should be forcibly removed from private houses and churches; portraits of saints painted in this manner should have the eyes gauged out and the icons thus defaced should be carried through the streets of the city. At the same time, the punishments to be meted out to any artist not honouring the old traditions, should be proclaimed aloud. Even during the Mass Patriarch Nikon preached a sermon, in the presence of the Tsar, about the unlawfulness of the new painting, which resembled the work of foreigners. He threw all outlawed icons on to the metal-plated floor, shattered them and ordered that they be burned.

The collision of old and new caused more unrest in 17th century Russia than anywhere else. It led to disputes between different groups of Russians, and the publication of numerous treatises about the concept of the icon, about the origin of art per se and about the artistic endeavours of Mankind. The tracts by Simon Ushakov, Simeon Polocky, Protopope Avakum, Karion Istomin and the Tsar Alexis Mihailovich himself, testify to the enormous importance placed on icon-painting at that time.

Once again victory went to the official ideology of the Russian Church, to which the Tsar himself subscribed. Again the claim was accepted, that: » the first artist is God himself; moved by the desire to create Man, he made him in his own image, both in face and form. And thus the *Urbild*, the prime image, of Man is God himself... Therefore the icon or image is no more than imitation. That is how the icon gets its name, for it is, by reason of the similarity, a relationship between the one visage and the other.« Simon Ushakov was also convinced that »God has granted to Man an intellectual power that is called imagination, which enables him to draw the shapes of different objects; He endows certain individuals – though not in equal measure – with the natural ability to create figures and forms and with the aid of various kinds of art to render visible the world that is in men's minds.«

In the 17th century there were still some icon-painters who, by virtue of their conviction and their gifts were elevated to membership of this élite circle of orthodoxy. Later, the educated class ceased to find any meaning in the old Byzantine exemplars, though these lived on until the 19th century in Christian folk-art.

The Forty Martyrs of Sebaste

Tempera on wood, 44 x 33.5 cm, legend in Greek, 11th century,
Ohrid (Macedonia), the icon gallery in the church of St Clement (Sveti Kliment).

The icon was probably painted for Ohrid cathedral, which is dedicated to St Sophia and in which the cult of the Forty Martyrs of Sebaste was followed with particular devotion. The entire cycle of scenes showing the warriors who – with one exception – died on the frozen lake, rather than renounce their faith, is also displayed in 11th century frescos in the north-west chapel of the St Sophia church (ground floor, near the altar). The crowning with victors' laurels, which Christ presents to the martyrs, is a symbolic scene of sacrifice and reward, which sums up the fundamental idea of this hagiography. This episode decorates the dome of the apse but is also presented as a single symbolic unity in the icon. The dating of the icon is suggested by the stylistic qualities, the way the naked bodies are modelled, the expression of agony through gestures, as well as the typical facial features and overlarge eyes.

The archangel Gabriel from the Annunciation

Tempera on wood with silver mountings, 111.5 x 67.5 cm, legend in Greek, early 12th century,
Ohrid (Macedonia) icon gallery of the Sveti Kliment church.

Together with the the icon of the Virgin this forms the composition of the Annunciation to the Virgin Mary, which once adorned the altar-screen of Sveti Kliment. The mountings of this icon were made from small silver plates. A number of ornaments and personages relevant to the subject are added to the central figure of the archangel: in the upper centre the throne was shown in readiness (it no longer exists), while figures of angels appear at each side. The date when this icon was painted is a matter of dispute among experts, because of the truly monumental central figure, and the relief-like folds of the garments around the body in motion contrasting with the very weak modelling of the amgel's face. It could have been painted in the late 11th century, but also in the 12th or even 13th century.

The Virgin from the Annunciation

Tempera on wood with mountings, 111.5 x 68cm, legend and donor's inscription in Greek. Early 12th century,
Ohrid (Macedonia), icon gallery of the Sveti Kliment church.

With the archangel Gabriel this icon forms the composition of the Annunciation to the Virgin, which once adorned the altar-screen of Sveti Kliment. The background and edges are covered in silver plates on which floral ornamentation, figures and the legend »God is with Thee« have been executed in chase-work. On the upper edge of the icon there are chased medallions with portrayals of Christ, Mary and St John (the Deisis), as well as Joachim and Anne, the parents of Mary. On the lower edge St Andrew and St Blaise are portrayed; on the sides are the prophets whose writings foretold the appearance of the Virgin Mary. This was the way the artist indicated the accordance between the Old and New Testaments. The decorative silver halo, the small enamel plates bearing the donor's inscription and the jewelry on the breast of the Virgin were added at a later date. The inscription on the vertical row of enamel plates reads: »Most holy of brides, I give Thee what is Thy due, Thy loyal servant, Leo, priest of God.« The poetic expression »priest of God« probably denotes the Archbishop of Ohrid, who in the early 12th century ordered that the icon, already painted, be given its silver cladding with an inscription. The weak modelling of the face contrasting with the strongly modelled garments – in which some 19th century retouching can be recognized – have led to different dates being suggested by experts: late 11th, 12th or 13th century.

Christic Pantocrator

Tempera on wood, 135 x 73 cm. Legend in Greek. 1262–63.
Ohrid (Macedonia), the icon gallery of the Sveti Kliment church.

This icon was donated by the archbishop Konstantin Kabasilas and an inscription on the back tells us the year in which it was painted: » This icon was painted in the year 1262–63, in the time of archbishop Konstantin Kabasilas.« On the left-hand edge of the picture there is a mysterious marking in cinnabar on a gold background. This could be a clue to the painter's identity: + XB. In the halo of the Pantocrator (Almighty) the Greek letters ON have been inscribed in the customary manner. They refer to a biblical quotation (Exodus 3, 14) which contains a definition of the Divinity: I AM THAT I AM. The unusual plasticity, the finely modelled face, the geometric regularity of the folds and the way the light is reflected from Christ's robe, all point to a painter who must have closely followed the current attempts in Constaninople to create a monumental style. However, in the painting of the drapery he resorted to older techniques.

John the Baptist ▷

Fresco. Legend and text of the scroll in Old Serbian. 1208–9. Studenica (former Yugoslavia),
church of St Mary, south side of the north-west pillar in the naos.

The shape and the framing of icons was often imitated in the frescos of medieval churches, when it was necessary to draw attention to the image of a particularly revered saint. An inscription on the drum of the dome of St Mary's church, in the monastery of Studenica, tells us that the frescos were painted in 1208–9. Some of the icons themselves are also painted in the fresco technique, including those beside the altar-screen and on the pillars in the west end of the naos. Here John the Baptist is shown prominently, as protector of mankind, holding a scroll with a text from the gospel (Matthew III, 2 and 10). John is also the patron saint of the founders of the monastery, Stefan and Sava, princes of the Serbian ruling dynasty, the Nemanjids.

The Raising of Lazarus ▷ ▷

Tempera on wood, 21.5 x 24 cm. Legend in Greek. 13th century. Athens, private collection.

This small icon illustrates one of the twelve great religious festivals. It is thought to have once been part of an altar-screen, as it was customary in Byzantine churches from the 11th century onward to hang icons of the feast-days on the architrave above the aisles leading to the altar. Its unusual background painted in cinnabar and other stylistic similarities lead art-historians to the view that it belonged with other festival icons, one of which, relating to the Transfiguration, is now in the Hermitage museum, St Petersburg. The dating of it to the 13th century is based on the strongly modelled and rounded body-shape under the clothing, the way the folds of the cloth are emphasised with long strokes, and the complexion and shape of the face with warm colours applied in broad, dense brush-strokes. The drawing of the face is reminiscent of Byzantine examples from the Comnenian period. However, the three-dimensional effect is achieved in a novel manner.

St James

Tempera on wood, 91 x 65 cm. Legend in Greek. 13th century.
From the monastery of St John the Evangelist, on the island of Patmos, Greece.
Details in the design of this icon indicate that it represents the ordination of the apostle James, the first bishop of Jerusalem; Christ is handing down a goblet from heaven and blessing the apostle. This is a theme that is seldom seen in icons. The period when the icon was painted has been established by stylistic comparisons with frescos at Sopocani and miniatures from the psalter in the monastery of Stavronikita on Mount Athos.

The Virgin Hodegetria (The Guide)

Mosaic on wood, 57 x 38 cm. Legend in Greek. Late 12th century. Monastery of Hilandar, Mount Athos, Greece.
This icon portrays the holy protectress of the Hilandar monastery: the Virgin Hodegetria. The work is executed in small cubes of coloured glass, in which a small gold plate is embedded. It is presumed that the icon was made in the final years of the 12th century, when Serbia's great ruling partnership of Stefan Nemanja and his son, the monk Sava, supervised work on the Hilandar monastery, which they founded on Mount Athos. As the church is dedicated to the Virgin Mary, the benefactor probably wanted to donate an icon which was as costly as he could afford. Large eyes and a severe, fixed gaze, the face staring fully to the front and drawn in precise detail, and tonal modelling of the drapery, whose folds do not exactly follow the contours of the body but nonetheless evoke its shape – these are the painterly qualities of the icon, which determine its attribution to a Constantinople workshop of the late 12th century.

St George

Tempera on wood, 145 x 86 cm. Legen and inscriptions in Greek. 1266–67. Struga (Macedonia), St George's church.
An inscription has been preserved on the back of this icon, naming the artist and the person who commissioned the work: »A gift of your servant, the humble deacon Jovan, who had the honour to be admitted to the service of the church; after I had sketched thy holy face with reverence, Jovan, who is well versed in the use of colours, painted this icon for me. Jovan sends his prayer (to you) with love in the year 1266–67, of the 5th indiction. Painted by the hand of the artist Jovan.« The commissioner of the picture, the deacon and referendary of the church of St Sophia, was a well-known art-lover. He probably ordered the icon from a local workshop, where Master Jovan worked in a very traditional manner. At all events there is no trace of the new style of art which came in with the restoration of the Byzantine Empire in 1261, under the Palaeologue dynasty.

St George

Tempera on wood, 109 x 72 cm. Legend in Greek. 13th century. Byzantine Museum, Athens.
The icon represents the figure, career and martyrdom of St George. The figure of the saint with halo and shield, executed in coloured relief, stands out from the rest of the painted surface. The benefactress, seen kneeling behind the warrior in the lower left-hand corner, has so far not been identified. Her name is not written anywhere, and with her tiny stature and her humble, adoring posture she further emphasises her nonentity. Although the icon was found in Kastoria, Greece, the military costume of St George, as well as the Kufic (early Arabic) inscription on his shield suggest that it was painted in the 13th century, either in Jerusalem or Cyprus, or in a workshop in the Balkans were the Latin influence was more significant. The painter has certainly followed the Byzantine tradition in his representation of the twelve scenes from the life of the saint, whereas the treatment of the figures shows certain Romanesque characteristics.

Virgin and Christchild

Tempera on wood, 89 x 59 cm. No legend. Around 1270–80.
Altar of the Hektorovic family in the cathedral of Hvar (Croatia).
It is generally supposed that this icon was painted in a workshop in Pisa, where Byzantine (and Comnenian) concepts of art were still current during the 13th century. With its lively colours and sharp contrasts, the facial expressions of Christ and the Virgin Mary, as well as the treatment of the garments, it is surely the work of a master for whom the striving for pictorial expression was more important than the canon of beauty founded on ancient tradition, which was still cultivated in Constantinople in the second half of the 13th century.

Crucifixion

Tempera on wood, 87 x 61.5 cm. 13th century. Byzantine Museum, Athens.

This is a processional icon, painted on both sides. On the rear side there is a 16th century portrayal of the Virgin and Christchild. The front, showing the crucifixion, has clearly been overpainted. Traces of the older painting can be recognized in the gold background with stars; this is thought to date from the 9th century. The more recent layer of painting, whose style gives it a 13th century date, depicts Christ, Mary and St John. Their faces, furrowed with pain and grief and surrounded by green shadows, are wonderfully portrayed. The harmonious proportions of the bodies, the clearly outlined forms under the folds of their garments, and the well-balanced tones of colour show the best qualities of the progressive school of Palaeologue painting in Constantinople from the second half of the 13th century.

Virgin and Christchild

Tempera on wood, severely damaged, with broken edges. Second half of the 13th century.
Monastery of Hilandar, Mount Athos, Greece.

This icon forms a pair with the icon of Christ Pantocrator, which has also been preserved in this Serbian monastic foundation; they were the principal icons of the altar-screen which was probably decorated for the first time in the second half of the 13th century. The painting shows exceptionally soft treatment of the face, perfect symmetry of the facial features, which radiate a cheerfulness almost suggestive of pagan antiquity, and a gentle blending of warm and cold colours. All this enables us to say that the icon reflects the concepts of beauty of those days, which found expression in the monumental deisis in mosaic on the gallery of the church of St Sophia in Constantinople.

42

The Virgin Hodegetria (The Guide)

Tempera on wood, with mountings, 97 x 67 cm. Second half of the 13th century.
Ohrid (Macedonia), icon gallery of the church of Sveti Kliment.

This is a processional icon with the crucifixion scene on the reverse side. It was found in the church where it is still kept today. Only the front has the silver chasing, showing the specially revered Virgin (with the title of Guide) with the Christchild. The background and frame of the icon are covered with small silver plates, which were made in a workshop where the craftsmen did not know what the end-use of their workmanship would be. Thus they deal with a variety of themes. Some show busts of saints, others scenes from the life of Christ - some repeated several times – or ornamentation, all in chased-work. On the lower edge one can even see a plate with the figures of the Virgin and Christ enthroned, containing the attribute »protectress.« In contrast to the older Byzantine icons, in which the the metal cladding is conceived as part of the thematic unity, here the costly chased-work is only an additional embellishment. The superbly executed oval, the symmetry of the facial features, and the soft nuances of ochre and green shading on the face, the potent combination of purple and green tones in the robes of the Virgin, are all marks of a gifted artist, though one who has remained nameless.

Crucifixion

Tempera on wood with canvas, 97 x 67 cm. Legend in Greek. Second half of the 13th century.
Ohrid (Macedonia), icon gallery of the Sveti Kliment church.

This crucifixion is painted on the reverse side of the processional ikon of the »Virgin Hodegetria.« The superb modelling of the face with muted greens and dense olive-green shading, the plasticity of the figures and the simplicity of the robes hanging down in great folds, the harmony of the cool blue, pale green and violet colours on a golden background –all these tell us that the masterly painter of this crucifixion was well-versed in the classicizing tendencies of Byzantine art in the second half of the 13th century. The grief of the Virgin Mary and St John is made clear not only in the formal gestures but even more in the facial expressions. This is further evidence of the return to ancient traditions in the so-called Palaeologue Renaissance.

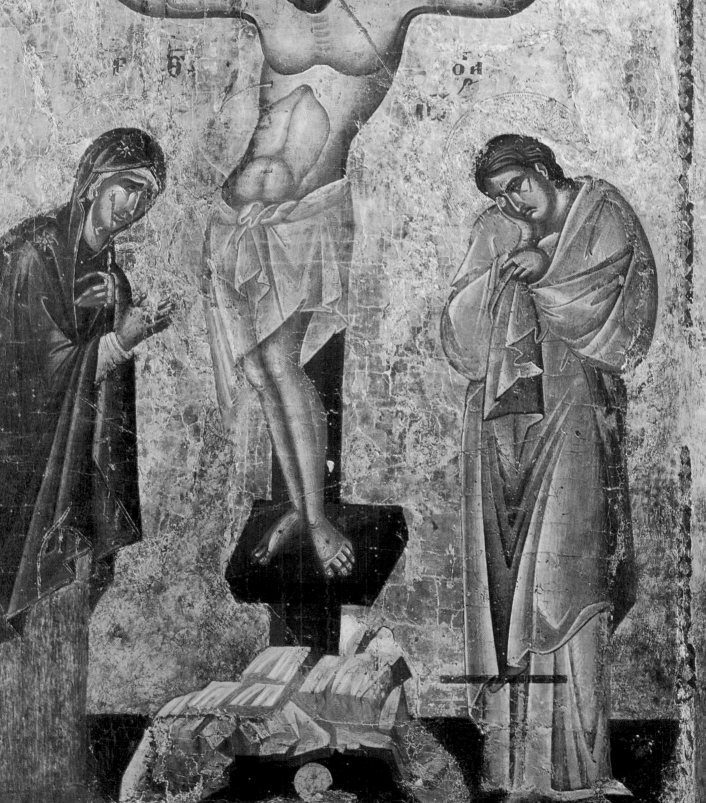

St Matthew the Evangelist

Tempera on wood, 115 x 56 cm. Legend in Greek. Late 13th or early 14th century.
Ohrid (Macedonia), icon gallery of the Sveti Kliment church.
We can see the hand of a master in the unusually fine painting of the figure of St Matthew, captured in movement – powerful, three-dimensional and nobly proportioned – and in the harmonious grading of the tones in the folds of his clothing. In the right-hand lower part of the icon, near the Evangelist's left foot, there is an inscription in Greek on an ochre background. No-one has been able to decipher it, but it may be the artist's signature. The icon's stylistic quality places it among the finest achievements of the mature period of Palaeologue art.

Ὁ ἉΓΙΟC   ΜΑΤΘΑΙΟ,

The Virgin Psychosostria (Redemptress)

Tempera on wood, with mountings, 94.5 x 80.3 cm. Legend in Greek. Early 14th century.
Ohrid (Macedonia), icon gallery of the Sveti Kliment church.

This processional icon carries the »Annunciation« on its reverse side. The background is covered with silver plates on which ornaments, busts of saints and texts in Greek have been executed in chased-work. The chased figures suggest a theme which is cleverly incorporated into the total composition: Christ as ruler of the world (on the upper edge), the prophets who foretold the appearance of the Virgin Mary (Aaron and Gideon on the right-hand edge, Daniel and Habakkuk on the left), and the saints (the righteous James, the New Testament patriarch, and St John Chrysostom, who is thought to have been added to the original chasing at a later date). This very richly decorated icon has a pendant in the representation of Christ as Redeemer. Both images were probably brought to Ohrid from Constantinople in the early 14th century at the request of Ohrid's archbishop Grigorije, to be placed in the St Sophia church. The Ohrid prelate was given the monastery of the Virgin Redemptress as a gift from the Byzantine emperor Andronikos II Palaiologos (1282–1328). The attribute of the Virgin which is emphasized in the Ohrid icon suggests that it was painted from the model of the dedicatory icon which is kept in the Constaninople monastery of the same name. The subtleties of colouring and the extraordinarily good modelling place both icons among the highest achievements of the mature Palaeologue period of Byzantine art. We can assume that they were painted in one of the Constantinople workshops in the early 14th century.

The contribution of archbishop Grigorije to the renovation of the St Sophia church was also an architectural one, and so there is every reason to assume that, through his connection with the metropolis, he was able to arrange for the transfer of the icons to Ohrid.

Annunciation

Tempera on wood, 94.5 x 80.3 cm. Legend in Greek. Early 14th century.
Ohrid (Macedonia), icon gallery of the Sveti Kliment church.

This image forms the reverse side of the processional icon »Virgin Psychosostria«. To judge from their stylistic features both sides were painted at the same time, although the reverse side was not given any silver chasing. This painting also has figures in movement, and an effect of depth is achieved in the painting of the archtectural background. The dark colours of the foreground contrast with the glowing light of the background and there is a gentle grading of colour in the faces. The icon probably comes from a Constantinople workshop and is among the best to have survived from the Palaeologue period of the early 14th century.

Christus Psychosostis (Christ the Redeemer)

Tempera on wood with chased silver, 96 x 70 cm. Legend in Greek. Early 14th century.
Ohrid (Macedonia), icon gallery of the Sveti Kliment church.
This processional icon has the »Crucifixion« on the reverse side. It was probably brought to Ohrid in the early 14th century on the instructions of archbishop Grigorije. The silver was apparently applied when the icon was painted but was damaged later. The background is covered with silver plates on which floral and geometric ornamentation has been chased. As in similar icons, the edges are decorated with busts of saints: Peter, Andrew, Paul, John the Evangelist, Matthew and Mark. The facial features are symmetrical, but weakly modelled. The hands are superbly drawn and the colours of the clothing harmonize well. The icon is clearly the work of an experienced artist, probably from a Constantinople workshop.

Crucifixion

Tempera on wood, 96 x 70 cm. Legend in Greek. Early 14th century,
Ohrid (Macedonia) icon gallery of the Sveti Kliment Church.

This is the reverse of the processional icon of »Christ the Redeemer«. The mastery of the artist is shown in the plasticity of the body of Christ, expressed in nuances of colour from grey-green to a light ochre, and in the transition from the dark shadows at the edge of the regular oval of the head to the pale highlghts of the chin and cheeks in the faces of the Virgin Mary and St John. Their elongated figures emphasize the foreground space which is enclosed by a painted wall. We can assume that this »Crucifixion« and the »Annunciation« on the reverse of the »Virgin Redemptress« were painted by one and the same artist in the early 14th century in a Constantinople workshop.

Ascension of Christ

Tempera on wood, 39.5 x 29 cm. Legend in Greek. About 1300.
Ohrid (Macedonia) icon gallery of the Sveti Kliment church.
It is generally assumed that this icon was specially painted for the Sveti Kliment church (where it was also found) in about 1300, as the church was decorated in 1295. The figures are represented gesticulating and in lively movement. It was obviously the painter's intention to stress the drama of these unusual events. This is especially clear in the contrasting and complimentary colours of the clothing and is most noticeable in the centre of the picture, where the Virgin and Christ in purple and dark blue against a background of gold appear separated from the other figures. The flesh-tones of the strongly-lit face, neck and elbows are painted with swift strokes in a very bright ochre. This technique suggests that the painter was able to work with a quick and sure hand. Indeed the icon is attributed to Michael or Eutichiotis, who have left their names on the frescos of this church and later worked in the service of the Serbian king Milutin. They are thought to typify the style described as the mature phase of Palaeologue art.

Crucifixion

Tempera on wood, 33.5 x 25.5cm. Legend in Greek. Chapel of the Annunciation on the island of Patmos, Greece.
This small icon probably belongs to a cycle illustrating the twelve great religious festivals on an altar-screen. The work is notable for the horizontal depiction of the event, the numerous details and individuals giving the event greater credibility, the plasticity in the treatment of the figures, whose body-shape is emphasized by the drape of their clothing, the lively gestures, the arrangement of the figures in a space enclosed by a wall, and the bright ochre tones which give relief-like emphasis to the faces and limbs. All this tells us that the painter of this icon worked in the tradtion of the Palaeologue artists.

Virgin with Christ-child

Temper on wood, 83 x 58cm. Legend in Greek. Early 14th century. Byzantine Museum, Athens.
Scholarly literature indicates that this image of the Virgin, with its asymmetry and expressiveness of the facial features, diverges very strongly from the classical canon of beauty as it was cultivated in Constantinople at the beginning of the 14th century. It is generally considered that this method of representation was only practised in workshops in Thessaloniki in the early 14th century and that this icon must therefore have come from there. The dating is based on an analysis of the forms and colours. The shadowing round the eyes and on the oval faces of the Virgin and Christ-child could almost be described as crudely painted, but it enhances the impression of plasticity, and the body-forms under the garments seem fairly solid. These features also point to an early 14th century date.

Virgin Episkepsis (Protectress)

Mosaic on wood, 95 x 62cm. Legend in Greek. Early 14th century. Byzantine Museum, Athens.
This icon came to Athens from Triglion in Bythinia (Asia Minor). It is made from relatively large mosaic-cubes made of coloured paste mixed with gold. The dating is based on stylistic evidence. The title of »Episkepsis« (Guardian, Protectress) does not designate any particular iconographic type of Virgin and Christ-child, but stresses her attribute of protecting and helping those who turn to her with their praryers and requests. In the 14th century images of the Virgin were more and more frequently given attributes which had already been proposed in Byzantine rhetoric and religious poetry.

Virgin Episkepsis (Protectress)

Detail. Tempera on wood, 103.5 x 52.5 cm. Legend in Greek. Mid-14th century.
Ohrid (Macedonia), icon gallery of the Sveti Kliment church.

The icon comes from the church of SS Cosmas and Damian in Ohrid. It portrays the Virgin in full length, holding Christ on her right arm. The angels in the medallions are Michael and Gabriel. They carry the instruments of Christ's future martyrdom. This allusion to the Passion of the Saviour, here expressed in vivid pictorial detail, tells us that this representation of the Virgin can be classed as what is known as the »Passion type.« The title »Episkepsis« (Guardian, Protectress) is again a reference to the human qualities ascribed to her in the poetry of the liturgy.

Virgin with Christ-child

Detail. Tempera on wood, 164.5 x 56 cm. Legend in Old Serbian. Circa 1350.
Altar-screen in Dečani, former Yugoslavia.

In Dečani five icons have survived on the altar-screen for which they were painted – a rare thing in any church. Since the frescos in Dečani church were commissioned by the benefactor, the Serbian king and later emperor Dušan (1331–1355) around the middle of the 14th century, it is assumed that the icons on the altar-screen were painted at the same time. The stylistic features of the icon, in which the Virgin and Child are captured in a movement which radiates tenderness, also point to 1350 as the approximate date of origin. The subtle combination of purple, cinnabar red and gold in relation to the cool nuances of green, the elongated proportions of the figures and the sure drawing of the body of the Virgin in movement – all single out the artist and his achievement from the many who were working in Serbia at that time.

Virgin with Christ-child

Tempera on wood with metal mounting, 91 x 53 cm. Legend in Greek, benefactor's inscription in Old Serbian.
Mid-14th century. Ohrid (Macedonia), icon gallery of the Sveti Kliment church.

This icon deviates from the Byzantine tradition in several respects: the red-haired Christ wears a greyish-white blouse with an unusually billowing collar. The Virgin's cloak is orange; in the drawing of the faces of mother and child Mediterranean rather than Byzantine influences are traceable; and the drawn-in eyelashes of the Virgin are quite unique. Even the silver chasing of the Virgin's halo, with its symbols of the Evangelists, deviates from the traditional mode of representation, since St Mark is represented by a double eagle. Standing figures of the prophets decorate the frame made of thin silver plates, in which ornaments have been executed in chased-work. Only at the bottom right-hand edge is there a small plate bearing a medallion, which does not belong to the orginal silver mounting. Originally the name and title of the man who had commissioned the work was entered in red paste: (Ni)KOLA (e)P(i)S(ko)P. Archbishop Nikola of Ohrid had probably ordered the icon from a Mediterranean master, who was working inland. For in Dečani, for example, artists from Kotor (Cattaro) on the Adriatic coast were working, and it appears that the Ohrid prelate had met this master through the Serbian court and ordered the icon from him.

Purification of the Virgin

Tempera on wood, 97 x 68.5 cm. Legend in Greek. Third quarter of the 14th century.
Ohrid, icon gallery of the Sveti Kliment church.

At a time when the exchange of artistic ideas between Constaninople and the Balkans was slowing down, the local workshops in each place were able to cover the domestic demand alone. This was true after 1346 in Serbia and Ohrid as well. It is probable that an artist in the third quarter of the 14th century painted this image of the festival of the Virgin on the reverse side of the large and solemn icon of the »Virgin Periblepta,« without diverging from the fixed rules of iconography. The colours and the draughtsmanship are those of an average painter who does not come near the standard of the master who painted the front of this processional icon.

The Archangel Michael, Great Taxiarch (commander of the celestial hosts)

Tempera on wood, 110 x 81.5 cm. Legend in Greek. Circa 1350–1360. Byzantine Museum, Athens.
It is presumed that this icon comes from the deisis group of an altar-screen. The title »Great Taxiarch« denotes the high rank of the archangel among the hosts of heaven. The cryptogram on the celestial sphere in the angel's hand has been deciphered as »Christ the just judge.« The technique of relief-like illumination of the forms by means of whole bunches of thin white lines is thoroughly typical of Byzantine icon-painting of the 1360s. The dating of this picture is based on this peculiarity of style.

St Nicholas calming the storm
(detail from: St Nicholas and his Vita)

Tempera on wood, 94.5 x 67 cm. Legend in Greek. Second half of the 14th century. Art Gallery, Skopje (Macedonia). This icon was found in the church of St Sophia in Ohrid. In a very unusual manner it portrays a large figure of the saint in the centre of the picture, while the scenes from his life are squeezed in around the edges. The detail shown here depicts one of the miracles attributed to St Nicholas as the patron saint of sailors. In its iconogrpahic details this event is also depicted in the traditional Byzantine style, as it had been passed down for centuries in word (the Vita) and picture (icon).

76

Diptych of the despot Yelena

Woodcut with silver and gold chasing, 7.7 x 6.5 cm. Text in Old Serbian.
Treasure-room of the monastery of Hilandar, Mount Athos, Greece.

This little icon consists of two panels (diptych), each a self-contained entity. In the centre of the right-hand panel the Virgin is surrounded by prophets, while on the left the figures of the Trinity are shown with the apostles. The busts of the prophets and apostles are surrounded by finely-carved tendrils. On the outside of the panels, chased in silver, is a lament for the death of an only son. Yelena, the wife of the despot Uglješa Mrnjavčevič, who lived in Seres, show- ed a particular interest in writing and especially in books. In her grief she wrote the text for this diptych and sent it to the Hilandar monastery, where her son was buried: »...Look down in Thy mercy, O Lord Jesus Christ, and Thou, O Queen and Mother of God, even on me in my affliction, so that I may always be concerned for the separation of my sould from my body, a separation which I saw in those who bore me, and in the child that I bore, and for the grief that burns eternally in my heart...« It is probable that the Metropolitan of Seres, Theodosius, presented the icon to the boy, and Yelena then had it set with pearls and gemstones and freshly mounted in gold and silver, before she sent it to Hilandar. In 1371 she lost her husband in the Battle of the Marica, and at the same time lost her home in Seres and her position as wife of an absolute ruler. Thereafter she lived as a nun under the name of Sister Yefimiya in the Serbian convent of Ljubostitum and later with Princess Milica at the Lazarevič court. Other literary texts by this first famous Serbian poetess have survived.

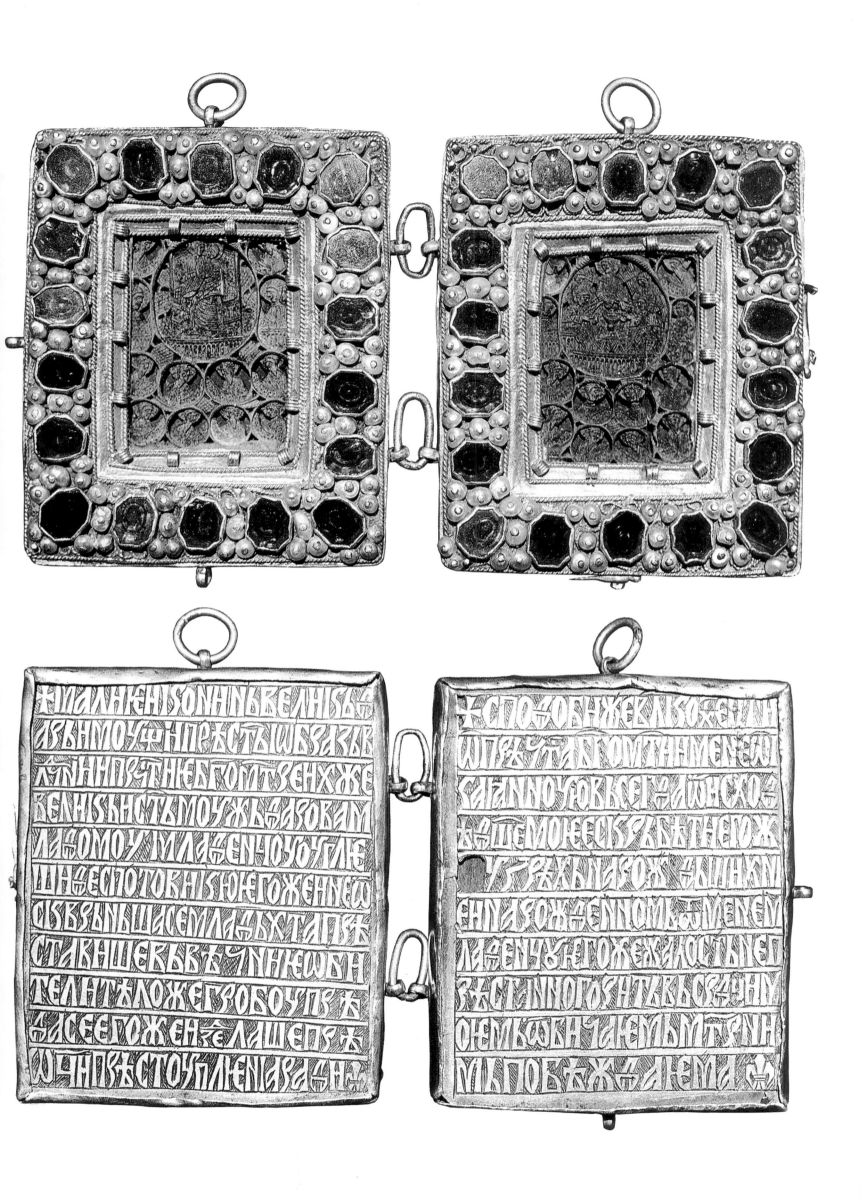

The Virgin Katafygi (Sanctuary) with St John the Evangelist

Tempera on Wood, 89 x 60 cm. Legend and donor's inscription in Greek.
Last third of the 14th century. National gallery, Sofia, Bulgaria.

This processional icon is painted on both sides. On the front the Virgin and St John the Evangelist are shown standing, while on the reverse side is the Vision of the Prophets Ezekiel and Habbakuk, a theme which echoes the 5th century mosaic which has been preserved in the apse of the Hosios David church in Salonika. On the front, between the figures of the Virgin and St John, the donor's inscription has been painted in cinnabar red. Originally it gave the full name of the aristocratic lady who had commissioned the work. All that can be read now is: »..Basilissa devoted servant of Christ the Lord.«

The icon was found in the monastery of Poganovo near Pirot, which was dedicated to John the Evangelist. It is possible, therefore, that the icon was made for the monastery, since it was not otherwise usual to depict the Virgin with John the Evangelist. This rare choice of the patron saint, and the attitude of the Virgin Mary with her head lowered and resting in her hand as though in a moment of deep grief, can only be explained by the influence of the patroness, a lady of high station. The attribute of the Virgin as »Katafygi« (Sanctuary) is also unusual on icons and indicates that the patroness was thoroughly familiar with liturgical poetry. This »Basilissa« may have been the wife of a despot, and was certainly a patrician and a connoisseur of the painting of her time. The extraordinary artistic value of this icon was recognized at a very early date; it is rightly considered to be one of the most beautiful works of the late Palaeologue style.

The Virgin Katafygi (Sanctuary)
(detail)

The Virgin is shown in her typical attitude of profound grief at the foot of the Cross. The epithet of »Sanctuary« does not appear to have any connection with the iconography of the Crucifixion scene; it can only be explained as an expression of the wish of the lady who commissioned the work, named as »Basilissa« in the Greek inscription.

Vita of St Mary of Egypt ▷

Tempera on wood, 25 x 29.5 cm. Legend in Greek. Late 14th century. Hilandar monastery, Mount Athos, Greece.
The life of St Mary of Egypt, probably recorded in the 7th century, is shown in four uninterrupted rows of images. Mary was a prostitute from Alexandria, who lived from the »oldest profession« until she was twenty-nine. When she saw pilgrims setting off in a ship bound for Jerusalem, she joined them out of pure curiosity, paying for her trip by offering her services to the crew. When she reached the Holy City, however, an angel prevented her from taking part in the church ceremonies. In desperation she turned to an icon of the Virgin, begged for forgiveness and promised to atone for her sins. She then crossed the river Jordan and went into the desert, where she lived as a hermitess for 47 years. As an old woman, now exhausted and humbled, she encountered the respected Egyptian monk Zosimus, who was deeply moved by her commitment to a life of virtue and gave her the Eucharist. When he returned on the same day the following year, he found her dead.
This Christian fable was often recorded in writing in the Middle Ages, but seldom made the subject of an icon. We can assume that the artist based his work on an illustrated life of the woman of Egypt. The stylistic features date the picture to the late 14th century, and it may have been the work of a Greek painter.

Vita of St Mary of Egypt ▷▷
(detail)

Mary, an elegantly dressed prostitute, asks the ship's captain to let her sail with the pilgrims to Egypt, and offers her services in return.

St Nahum

Tempera on wood, 91.5 x 70.5 cm. Legend in Greek. Second half of the 14th century.
Ohrid (Macedonia), icon gallery of the Sveti Kliment church.

This processional icon has a bust of St Nahum on the front. On the reverse there is a much later painting of the archangel Michael, probably done in the 18th century. As saints, educators and Slavonic writers, Kliment and Nahum were highly revered in Ohrid and the surrounding region. There are many frescos and icons which testify to their cult in the Middle Ages, and this icon is one of them. It was found in the church of the Virgin of Lazaret in Ohrid, so we can assume it was painted for an Ohrid church. The dating is based on stylistic features.

St Kliment

Tempera on wood, 86 x 65.5 cm. Legend in Greek. Late 14th or early 15th century.
Ohrid (Macedonia), icon gallery of the Sveti Kliment church.
The Slavonic saint Kliment was greatly venerated both in the churches of Ohrid and in the entire archbishopric. This portrayal of the saint on an Ohrid processional icon, only one of many to have survived, is the work of a skilled artist, whose tendency to idealize, spiritualize and stylize his subject is derived from the tradition of Byzantine icon-painting at the turn of the 15th century.

Jesus Christ, Saviour and Giver of Life

Tempera on wood, 131 x 88.5 cm. Legend and inscription in Greek. 1393–94, Art Gallery, Skopje, Macedonia.
This icon was part of the altar-screen of the monastery cathedral of Zrze in Macedonia (former Yugoslavia). It is dated by an inscription in Greek on the upper edge of the picture: »This icon of Our Lord Jesus Christ was painted in the year 1393–94.« There are also some traces of writing on the lower edge. The painter of this icon was the Metropolitan Jovan-Zograph, a famous prelate and artist, whose forefathers administered the monastery and their family estates in the village of Zrze. Jovan-Zograph also painted the signed frescos in the church of St Andrew on the Treska. This educated and gifted painter left works which show how he strove, in the difficult times of the Turkish invasions, to follow the progressive trends in the painting of the Constantinople school, which in those years tended towards strongly modelled, monumental figures. Typical of this style are the bunches of pale, short lines, and gentle transitions from dark shadowing to pale ochre in the face, neck and hands. These features place Jovan-Zograph in the tradition of late Palaeologue art.

St Demetrius

Tempera on wood, 34.5 x 26.5 cm. Legend in Greek. 15th century.
Museum of Applied Art, Belgrade, Serbia/Yugoslav Republic.
The icon shows the warrior-saint in his armour, to which the artist devotes much attention. Fresco-painters in Serbian monasteries of the 15th century also liked to depict soldiers in full equipment. The splendid colouring and harmonious proportions, as well as the manner of the modelling, support a 15th century dating.

St Sava and St Simeon

Tempera on wood, 32.5 x 26 cm. Legend and text of scroll in Old Serbian. 15th–16th century.
National Museum, Belgrade, Serbia/Yugoslav Republic.

The two oldest saints of Serbia, St Simeon (formerly the ruler Stefan Nemanja) and his son, St Sava (first archbishop of the independent Serbian Church) were represented together in Serbian church frescos as early as the beginning of the 14th century. The fact that the founder of the Nemanjid dynasty and state and the founder of the archbishopric (1219) were portrayed side by side, can be attributed to the influence of the Serbian Church and the wish of its learned archbishops to defend and assert their independence from the Byzantine Church through the glorification of their native saints. The cult of St Simeon, which began as early as the first years of the 13th century, and of St Sava, who was revered as soon as he died in 1235, was practised paricularly in the monastery of Hilandar, whose renowned founders they were. Scholarly sources place this icon in the 15th or 16th century by virtue of its stylistic features.

The Virgin Pelagonitissa

Tempera on wood, 134 x 93.5 cm. Legend in Greek, inscription in Old Serbian. 1421–22.
Art Gallery, Skopje, Macedonia.

The icon was originally part of the iconostasis of the katholikon in the monastery of Zrze. The well-preserved inscription on the upper edge reads: »For the sake of Our Lord, God and Saviour, Jesus Christ, and by the grace of the immaculate Virgin, this holiest of visages was painted in the year 1421–22. Remember, Lord, Thy holy monk Kyrios Makarije-Zograph.« On the lower edge is a second insciption, which mentions the patron and his family: »Prayer of the servant of God Konstantin, son of Djurdjič and grandson of Schagman and of his wife Kyra Theodora, and of the sons Jakob and Kalojan and Dmitar and of the daughters Anna and Jela. Remember also, God, his parents and his brother Bogoje, who died in prison and his daughter Kyra Zoe.« Makarije-Zograph was, as we know from other sources, the brother of the Metropolitan Jovan-Zograph and a descendent of the family who founded the monastery in the mid–14th century. When the Turks invaded Macedonia he went to work in the monastery of Ljubostinja, but later returned home. For the iconostasis in Zrze monatery, which had been renovated by the Djurdjič family, Makarije painted the Virgin and Christ-child – an icon which bears the epithet »Pelagonitissa« and shows the child playing in his mother's arms. Since many surviving icons repeat this iconographic type and this attribute, we can assume that in Pelagonia there existed a very old, revered and widely-known icon of the Virgin and Christ-child, which was given the epithet of its place of origin. All later copies retain the basic outlines of the original image. The »Virgin Pelagonitissa« painted by Makarije-Zograph is distinguished by its very dark flesh-tints and stylized facial features. It is a manner of painting with which artists of the 15th century strove to idealize and spiritualize sacred figures. The three-dimensional shape of the body was ignored and only the contours were emphasized. Despite the inadequate knowledge of anatomy and the exaggerated care with which the clothing is reproduced, Makarije proves himself to be an icon-painter who was familiar with works of greater artistic quality and attempted to learn from their example.

The Petrovskaya Virgin

Tempera on wood, with metal chasing, 31 x 25.5 cm. Legend in Greek. 15th century.
Museum in the monastery of the Holy Trinity, Zagorsk, Russia.

This is a typical example of a small prayer-icon, which was in private ownership and was brought to the monastery when the owner died. It is known that this icon belonged to Princess Paraskova, the second wife of Prince Daniel Borisovich Promkov-Rostovski, who was buried in 1582 in Zagorsk's Sergei-Lavra monastery. Stylistic features lead to the conclusion that the icon was painted in a Moscow workshop, where in the 15th century it was customary to paint the flesh in dark brown tones and the main expression was in the delineation.

Christ Emmanuel

Tempera on wood, with metal chasing, 26 x 21 cm. Legend in Old Russian.
Museum in the monastery of the Holy Trinity, Zagorsk, Russia.

This small prayer icon came to the monastery of the Holy Trinity in 1556 when its owner was buried. It had belonged to Feodor V. Korobov, who was present at the marriage of Ivan the Terrible to Anastasia Romanovna in 1547. Its style indicates that it was painted in the 15th century in a Moscow workshop. The consistent stylization of the figures, the accent on delineation and the neglect of three-dimensional volume are among the typical mannerisms of Russian painters of that period. The master of the icon of »Christ Emmanuel« only emphasizes the eyes and draws the observer's attention to them, so that he is distracted from the material world and drawn into the abstract spheres of dogma.

Virgin and Christ-child

Tempera on wood, 79 x 47 cm. No legend. 15th–16th century.
Art Gallery, Skopje, Macedonia.

This processional icon was found in the church of St Nicholas in Prilep. It is a good example of a particular type of portrayal of the Virgin, practised in the province of Pelagonia. Scholarly sources also refer to this type of Virgin and Child as »Vzigranije mladenca« (Playing with the Child). The anonymous artist, who probably painted this picture for a church in Pelagonia, perhaps even for the St Nicholas church in Prilep, was not a sklled master. The artist has not been able to depict successfully the body of the baby Jesus in playful movement, not does the calm figure of the mother show any convincing anatomical sjape under the clothing. The folds of the material are covered with numerous thin lines; however, these do not show the contours of the human body but only serve as decoration of the flat surface. Nonetheless, the artist achieves a certain monumentality, thanks to the enlarged figures of Mary and Christ, which occupy almost the whole painted area, and the tiny figures of angels which bow in reverence to the Virgin from the segments in the upper corners of the picture. The exaggerated plasticity of the bare limbs of the sacred figures, compared to the two-dimensional treatment of the clothed parts, reveal an unskilled and poorly educated provincial painter, though one not lacking in a fresh naivety. If one compares this icon with the »Virgin Pelagonitissa« (today in the National Musuem, Belgrade) dating from the second half of the 14th century, one can see that the classical style in icon-painting of the early 14th century had made no impression on the folk-art of isolated provincial workshops.

The Raising of the Oxen of Glicarius
A scene from the icon of the Vita of St George

Tempera on wood, 134 x 74.5 cm.legend in Greek. 15th–16th century. Church of St George, Struga, former Yugoslavia.
The scene depicted here is just one episode in the detailed representation of the life of St George, which is grouped round the large standing figure of the saint in the centre of the icon. This picture refers to one of the miracles ascribed to St George, who was venerated as the patron saint of farmers.

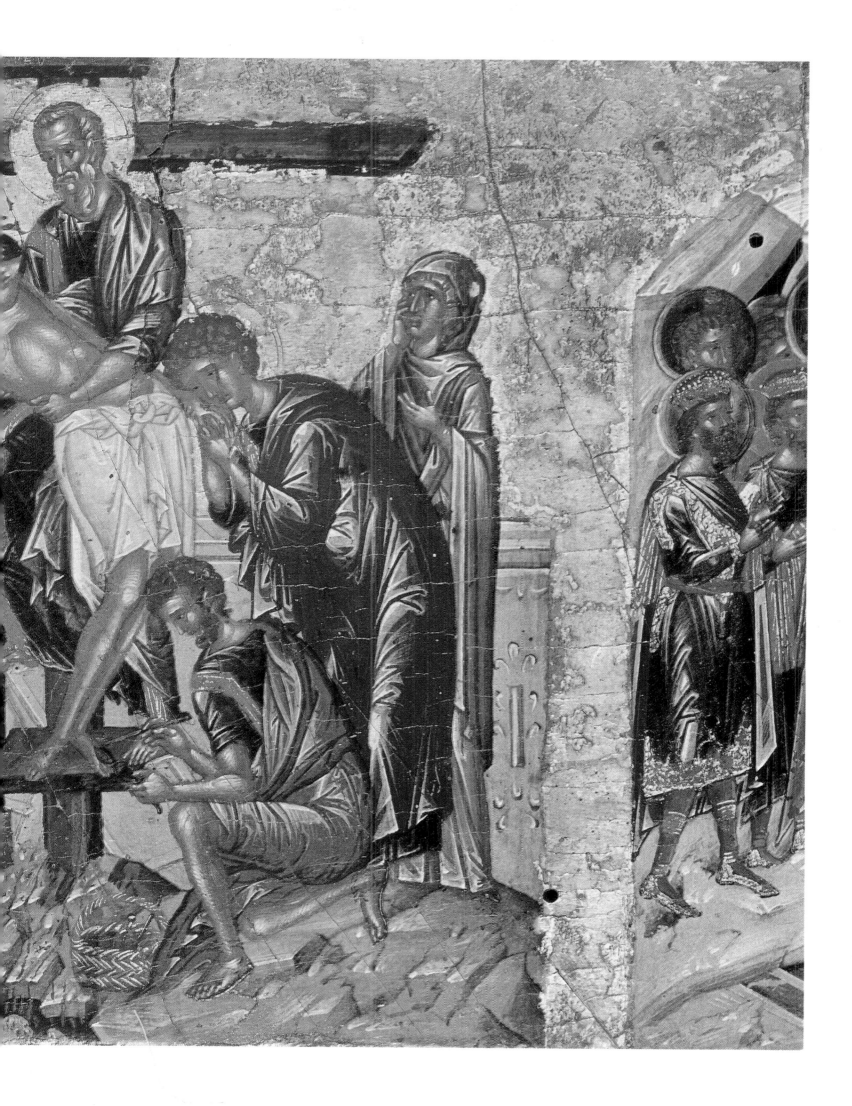

The Vladimirskaya Virgin

Tempera on wood, with gold and silver chasing, 32.5 x 25.5 cm. Legend in Greek. Early 16th century.
Museum in the Holy Trinity Church, Zagorsk, Russia.

This is a prayer-icon which was in private hands until it came to the Holy Trinity monastery in 1514. It belonged to Grigoriye Romanovich Zastolbski and was given the name »Vladimirskaya« because it belongs to the same iconographic type as the famous Russian icon, »The Virgin of Vladimir,« which was highly revered as early as the 12th century. As was customary, this little prayer-icon is richly mounted with small gold and silver plates on which ornamentation has been added in chased-work and filigree. Pearls were used as additional decoration. It is the work of an unnamed artist trained in the Byzantrine tradition of icon-painting.

116

Coronation of St George

Tempera on wood, 80 x 53.5 cm. Legend in Greek. 16th century. National Gallery of Art, Plovdiv, Bulgaria.
The coronation of the canonized warrior and martyr is a very popular theme of later Byzantine painting. An angel comes as a messenger from heaven bringing the wreath which he places on the head of the martyr with the blessing of Christ, a reward for his deeds in the hereafter. The iconographic formula of such pictures dates back to the ancient world, but it continues to appear in frescos or icons depicting the lives of saints, whenever there is a need to emphasize steadfast faith even to martyrdom. The Plovdiv icon represents this traditional theme and recalls St George's refusal to serve in the army led by the Roman emperor. From the Comnenian period onward icons of this kind continued to depict the saintly warrior very frequently, even in the post-Byzantine period.

Virgin Keharitomeni (Full of Grace)

Tempera on wood, 106 x 83 cm. Legend in Greek. 16th century Museum of the Holy Synod, Sofia, Bulgaria.
The icon represents the Virgin and Christ-child as well as eight scenes from her Vita and the Deisis on the upper border. The attribute »Full of Grace« is one of the usual epithets which, in the early centuries of Christianity, was adopted from Byzantine liturgical poetry and used in icons and frescos. In this case it is a processional icon. The groove for a pole is visible on the lower edge. It is painted on both sides. On the reverse side is a »Crucifixion.« The painter probably took a good traditional icon as his model, but he has turned the folds of the robe into crudely drawn ornamentation, and the shading of the face stands out too strongly from the sharply lit surfaces.

Birth of the Virgin Mary
(detail)

The scene represents the celebration of the birth of Mary and is part of the usual cycle of pictures from the Vita of the Virgin. The presentation of gifts to her mother Anne, the bathing of the new-born and the cradle are the traditional details of this episode which had been depicted in this way in Byzantine art for hundreds of years.

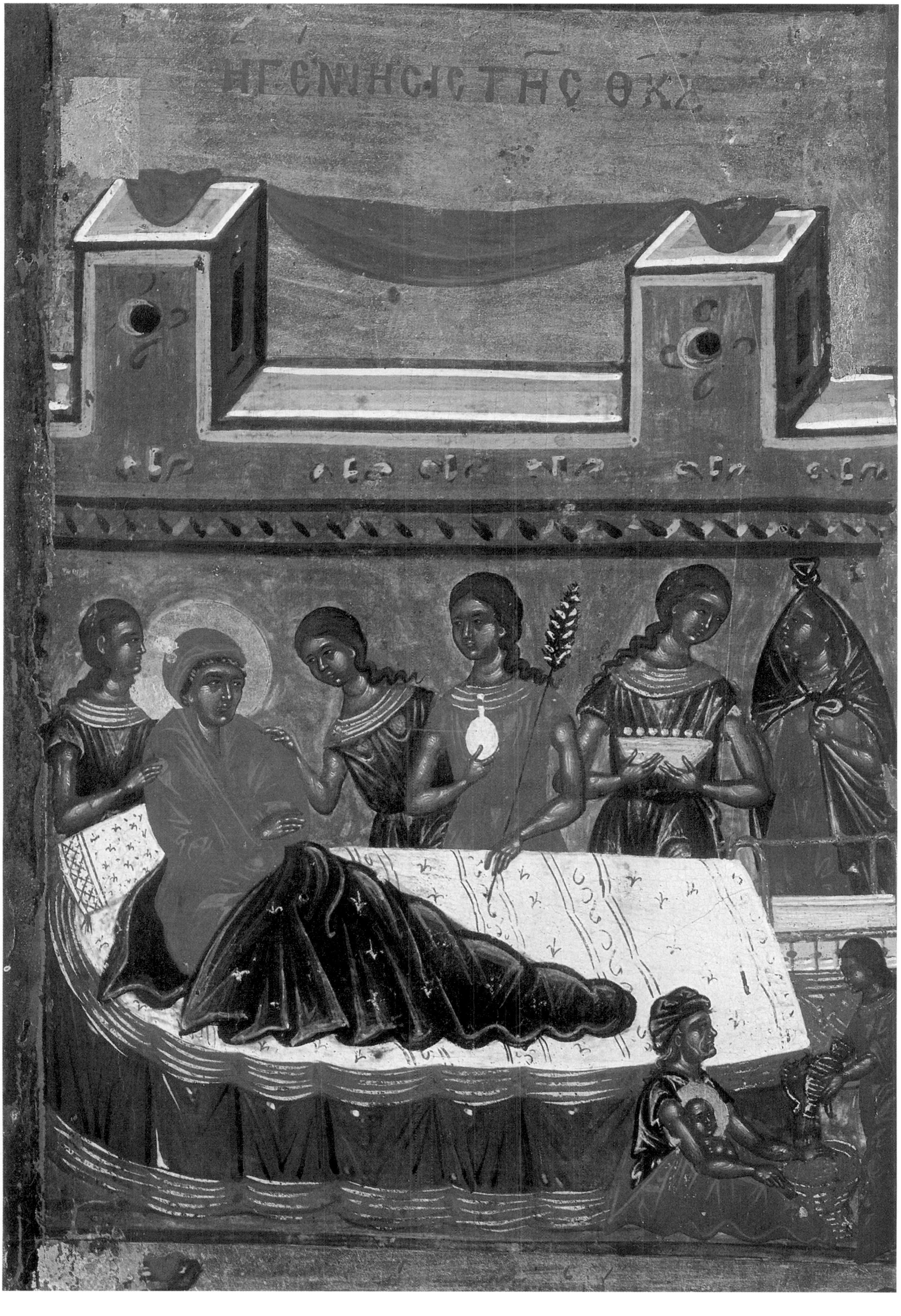
Η ΓΕΝΝΗΣΙΣ ΤΗΣ ΘΚ

Iconostasis

Tempera on wood with woodcuts. Legend in Old Serbian. 1620. Hilandar monastery, Mount Athos, Greece.
The door comes from the chapel of St Tryphon, situated outside the walls at the entrance of the monastery. The work on this iconostasis, which is richly decorated with wood-carving, was shared between archdeacon Isaia, archdeacon Mihailo and the monk Georgiye Mitofanovič. Georgiye painted the icons and the images on the door to the chancel. In 1620, when this work was completed, he reached the pinnacle of his artistic achievement. The balance of his palette, the modelling of the flesh on the faces of the saints, the drawing and proportions of the figures show this altar door to be to be one of the finest of this master's late works. His entire output was very extensive. Many of his icons and frescos have been preserved in Herzogovina, in Dalmatia and in Serbia, where he worked in 1615–16 and 1620.

Head of the Virgin
(detail)

On the door which gave the priests access to the chancel, the Annunciation to the Virgin was depicted in Byzantine art from the Comnenian period onward, and perhaps earlier. Georgiye Mitrofanovič, the monk and artist of the Hilandar monastery, observed this tradition when he repeated the theme in the St Tryphon chapel. The busts of David and Solomon also form part of this traditional iconography. Georgiye's style and technique indicate that he was a close follower of the work of the so-called Italo-Cretan and Italo-Greek painters, who were considered the most advanced in the eastern Christian world.

Crucifix

Carved and painted in tempera on wood, 197 x 187 cm. Legend in Old Serbian. 16th century.
Church of John the Baptist in Slepče, former Yugoslavia.

In many Orthodox churches crucifixes have been preserved on the altar-screens. In the 16th century they were usually carved in wood, then painted and decorated with gold. They represent the crucifixion of Christ, but often – as in this example – the symbols of the Evangelists are found on the arms of the cross, beside the body of Christ. In many workshops in the Balkans and Mount Athos similar crucifixes were produced as elements of the screen in front of the high altar. In addition, special plaques were placed below the cross containing the images of the Virgin and St John the Evangelist. The Slepče crucifix is a work of this type, but is exceptional because of its very fine carving and the warm colours of the well-preserved painted surfaces.

John the Baptist

Tempera on wood, 63.3 x 42.5 cm. Legend and inscription in Serbian. 1644.
Museum of the Serbian Orthodox Church, Belgrade.

This icon comes from the Krusedol monastery in Syrmium. It represents John the Baptist with wings and holding in his left hand a bowl containing his own head. In the same hand is a tall cross. All these attributes, as well as the saint's angelic appearance, have their origin in iconographic precedents which were popular as early as the end of the 13th century, and were influenced by Byzantine liturgical poetry. In the lower part of this icon two texts can be recognized. The one on the scroll has the words of the hymn which was sung in procession to Vespers on the night before the festival of the Beheading of John the Baptist. The other, written around the scroll, gives information about the date when the picture was painted and about the person who donated it: »Completed on 29th November of the year 1644. The donor is the most reverend Metropolitan of Belgrade and Syrmium Kyr Ilarion. God bless him!«

St Marina

Tempera on wood, and woodcut. Legend in Bulgarian. 17th century. Museum of the Holy Synod, Sofia, Bulgaria.
The art of woodcarving was highly developed in Balkan workshops in the late Middle Ages. In particular, the doors to the high altar and the crucifixes on the altar-screens were decorated with carved floral or geometric decorations, which were then painted and gilded. This painting of St Marina is one of these altar doors. Since the Middle Ages the saint had been frequently depicted as a protectress against evil and demonic powers and was featured in the decoration of several altar doors.

132

St Anne and the Virgin Mary

Tempera on wood, 106 x 67 cm. Legend in Greek. 1637. Benaki Museum, Athens.
The icon is signed and dated in the inscription. It was painted by Emanuel Canesa and shows how the traditional forms persisted in Greek workshops around the Mediterranean, especially in Crete. The so-called Italo-Cretan masters continued, after the fall of Byzantium, to supply Orthodox patrons with icons, right up to the 18th century. We can see that it is only in this late period that Baroque forms began to appear in the iconography. The flower which the child Mary is holding in her hand as a symbol of Christ, is a far from usual motif and shows the painter's desire to innovate. However, the manner of painting and design, the attitude of the mother and child and the combination of colours show Canesa to be a loyal follower of the Old Masters of Byzantine art.

134

Entry of Christ into Jerusalem

Tempera on wood, 22.5 x 35.5 cm. Legend in Old Serbian. 1577–78 Lomnica monastery, Bosnia-Herzogovina.
From the signature of the artist, Longinus, who painted the iconostasis of the principal church (katholikon) of the Lomnica monastery, we can see that he completed this work in 1578–79. The icon has recently been cleaned and returned to its original place in the monastery. In the lower row there are two large principal icons: The Virgin with the Christ-child, Angels and Prophets, and an icon of Christ. In the upper row the Christian festivals are illustrated in smaller pictures. One of these is the »Entry of Christ into Jerusalem« (the Palm Sunday festival) shown here. Master Longinus was a monk in the monastery of Peč, a poet and much in demand as an icon-painter. He worked in Peč, Decani, Piva, Velika Hoca and for other churches in the re-established patriarchate of Peč. After 1557, the patriarchate exerted a lively influence over the cultural life of Serbia, since the religious tolerance of the Ottoman empire had made possible a renewed blossoming of icon-painting in the Serbian lands. Longinus, who was active in the centre of Serbian monasticism, drew his painting largely from examples of Serbian iconography of the early 14th century. His method of composition, which is usually completed by a high mountain or by some architectural feature, as well as his traditional arrangement of the dark-cloaked figures in the foreground in front of the pale-coloured mountain slopes, or against a background of ochre or gold and the fine modelling of the faces with light shadowing and fresh colours – all these characteristics distinguish Longinus as a gifted exponent of icon-painting in Serbia in the late 16th century.

St George slaying the Dragon

Tempera on wood, 88 x 63 cm. Inscription in Bulgarian. 1667. Art Gallery, Sofia, Bulgaria.
This icon comes from the monastery of Kremikovac. The inscription on the dark background mentions everyone who was concerned with the commissioning of the icon: » This picture was painted at the order of Abbot Kyr Basilius in the year 1667. Remember, Lord, the servants of God, the donors Petko, Peter and Theodor.« In those days it often happened that several benefactors collaborated in commissioning an icon. The painter of this picture probably had rather limited artisitic skill, but a sure feel for fresh, pure colours. He presents in the traditional manner St George slaying the dragon and freeing the princess.

Part of the iconostasis in St Michael's church ▷

Szentendre, Hungary.

In the Eastern Orthodox churches in the 18th century very high wooden iconostases were built and decorated with icons and wood-carvings. The iconostasis illustrated here from the Serbian »Počarevacka« church in Szentendre has been decorated with six throne-icons, by unknown artists, on the lower level, and above them the Deisis with twelve icons of the apostles. Above that are sixteen icons of the prophets and the whole is crowned with a crucifixion scene and the painted images of the Virgin Mary and John the Evangelist. The iconostasis consists of eighteen medallions illustrated with the Stem of Jesse and the Prophets. According to Byzantine iconography this traditional composition on the altar-doors must precede the representations of the Annunciation and Baptism on the wings of the iconostasis. The Baroque form of the tendrils which link the medallions together, as well as Baroque elements on the painted surfaces herald a new epoch in Serbian art and the tentative turning to a new concept of art which was not Byzantine, but which had long been current in western Europe.

Part of a templon with the saints Elias, Yelisa and Theodor ▷▷

Tempera on wood, and wood-carving. Legend in Greek. 17th century.
Museum of the Holy Synod, Sofia, Bulgaria.

As the Middle Ages drew to an end, iconostases in the Balkans were often embellished with carving, gilding and ornamental reliefs. The part of this templon, that is to say the painted wooden panel above the iconostasis, represents a number of holy warriors on horseback. The clumsily drawn animals, the faulty proportions of figures, architecture and landscape and the schematically drawn faces are the work of an ordinary craftsman who had only the barest training in painting, yet the freshness and purity of his colours and his sense of the decorative no doubt appealed to the taste of his patron and contemporaries.

St Michael the Archangel ▷▷▷

Tempera on wood, with a carved wooden frame, 61 x 43 cm. Legend in Old Serbian. 1742.
Church of St Michael (also known as »Počarevacka«), Szentendre, Hungary.

Un unknown painter created this picture for the iconostasis of the Serbian »Počarevacka« church dedicated to the Archangel Michael, in Szentendre. Since all the icons on this large altar-screen are very similar, it is assumed that the date of 1742 given on the icon of the »Nativity« refers to the erection and decoration of the whole iconostasis. The influence of Baroque stylistic elements can be seen in these icons. Presumably these influences were brought by the Serbs from Wallachia as far as the Serbian diocese of Buda, for the Serbs maintained relations with Rumania and followed the developments of Rumanian sacred art in Rumania during the Brankoveanu epoch.